Adobe® Acrobat® X Pro

Level 1

Adobe® Acrobat® X Pro : Level 1

Part Number: 084548
Course Edition: 1.0

NOTICES

DISCLAIMER: While Element K Corporation takes care to ensure the accuracy and quality of these materials, we cannot guarantee their accuracy, and all materials are provided without any warranty whatsoever, including, but not limited to, the implied warranties of merchantability or fitness for a particular purpose. The name used in the data files for this course is that of a fictitious company. Any resemblance to current or future companies is purely coincidental. We do not believe we have used anyone's name in creating this course, but if we have, please notify us and we will change the name in the next revision of the course. Element K is an independent provider of integrated training solutions for individuals, businesses, educational institutions, and government agencies. Use of screenshots, photographs of another entity's products, or another entity's product name or service in this book is for editorial purposes only. No such use should be construed to imply sponsorship or endorsement of the book by, nor any affiliation of such entity with Element K. This courseware may contain links to sites on the Internet that are owned and operated by third parties (the "External Sites"). Element K is not responsible for the availability of, or the content located on or through, any External Site. Please contact Element K if you have any concerns regarding such links or External Sites.

TRADEMARK NOTICES Element K and the Element K logo are trademarks of Element K Corporation and its affiliates.

Adobe® Acrobat X Pro is a registered trademark of Adobe Systems Inc., in the U.S. and other countries; the Adobe products and services discussed or described may be trademarks of Adobe Systems Inc. All other product names and services used throughout this course may be common law or registered trademarks of their respective proprietors.

Copyright © 2011 Element K Corporation. All rights reserved. Screenshots used for illustrative purposes are the property of the software proprietor. This publication, or any part thereof, may not be reproduced or transmitted in any form or by any means, electronic or mechanical, including photocopying, recording, storage in an information retrieval system, or otherwise, without express written permission of Element K, 500 Canal View Boulevard, Rochester, NY 14623, (585) 240-7500, (800) 478-7788. Element K Courseware's World Wide Web site is located at **www.elementkcourseware.com**.

This book conveys no rights in the software or other products about which it was written; all use or licensing of such software or other products is the responsibility of the user according to terms and conditions of the owner. Do not make illegal copies of books or software. If you believe that this book, related materials, or any other Element K materials are being reproduced or transmitted without permission, please call (800) 478-7788.

Your comments are important to us. Please contact us at Element K Press LLC, 1-800-478-7788, 500 Canal View Boulevard, Rochester, NY 14623, Attention: Product Planning, or through our Web site at **http://support.elementkcourseware.com**.

Adobe® Acrobat® X Pro : Level 1

Lesson 1: Accessing PDF Documents

A. Open PDF Documents 2

B. Explore the Adobe Acrobat X Pro Interface 5

C. Browse Through PDF Documents 13

Lesson 2: Creating PDF Documents

A. Create PDF Documents from a File............................ 22

B. Create a PDF Document Using the Print Command 29

C. Create a PDF Document from Web Pages 32

D. Create a PDF Document Using Email Applications.............. 36

E. Create a PDF Document Using Acrobat 41

Lesson 3: Navigating to a Specific Content in a PDF Document

A. Perform a Search 52

B. Manage Bookmarks.. 57

C. Work with Links 65

Lesson 4: Updating PDF Documents

A. Manipulate PDF Document Pages 74

B. Edit Content in a PDF Document 83

C. Add Page Elements 89

D. Extract Content from a PDF Document 95

Lesson 5: Working with Multiple PDF Documents

A. Control Access to Multiple PDF Documents 104

B. Search Multiple PDF Documents   112

Lesson 6: Reviewing PDF Documents

A. Initiate a Review   122

B. Review a PDF Document   129

C. Compare PDF Documents.   138

Lesson 7: Validating PDF Documents

A. Sign a PDF Document Digitally   144

B. Verify a Digital ID   155

Lesson 8: Converting PDF Files

A. Optimize PDF Files.   160

B. Convert PDF Files to Other Formats   166

Appendix A: Setting Scanner Preferences

A. Scan a Document.   172

Lesson Labs.   177

Solutions   187

Glossary   189

Index   191

About This Course

You may have used different applications to create documents for your own reference. However, you may now want to share your files electronically by email, over a network, or on the web, so that recipients can view, print, and offer feedback. In this course, you will use Adobe® Acrobat® X Pro to make your information more portable, accessible, and useful to meet the needs of your target audience.

Adobe® Acrobat® X Pro removes the constraints of proprietary file formats, enabling you to provide information in a universally accessible format, and at the same time, ensuring that your audience can view and interact with the file as you intended. It is a perfect tool to create, control, and distribute secure and high-quality Adobe PDF documents.

Course Description

Target Student

This course is for individuals with little or no experience using Adobe Acrobat Pro, but who need to create and share PDF files and PDF Portfolios. Students may have experience using office productivity applications, such as a word processor or spreadsheet program, but with little or no experience using a robust database.

Course Prerequisites

Basic experience with computers and exposure to Microsoft Office applications, such as Word and Excel.

Course Objectives

In this course, you will use Adobe® Acrobat® X Pro to create and manage PDF documents.

You will:

- Access information in a PDF document.
- Create PDF documents.
- Navigate to and search for a specific content in a PDF document.
- Update PDF documents.
- Work with multiple PDF documents.

- Review a PDF document.
- Validate a PDF document.
- Optimize and convert PDF documents to other formats.
- Set the scanner preferences and scan a document.

How to Use This Book

As a Learning Guide

This book is divided into lessons and topics covering a subject or a set of related subjects. In most cases, lessons are arranged in order of increasing proficiency.

The results-oriented topics include relevant and supporting information you need to master the content. Each topic has various types of activities designed to enable you to practice the guidelines and procedures as well as to solidify your understanding of the informational material presented in the course.

At the back of the book, you will find a glossary of the definitions of the terms and concepts used throughout the course. You will also find an index to assist in locating information within the instructional components of the book.

In the Classroom

This book is intended to enhance and support the in-class experience. Procedures and guidelines are presented in a concise fashion along with activities and discussions. Information is provided for reference and reflection in such a way as to facilitate understanding and practice.

Each lesson may also include a Lesson Lab or various types of simulated activities. You will find the files for the simulated activities along with the other course files on the enclosed CD-ROM. If your course manual did not come with a CD-ROM, please go to **http://www.elementk.com/courseware-file-downloads** to download the files. If included, these interactive activities enable you to practice your skills in an immersive business environment, or to use hardware and software resources not available in the classroom. The course files that are available on the CD-ROM or by download may also contain sample files, support files, and additional reference materials for use both during and after the course.

As a Teaching Guide

Effective presentation of the information and skills contained in this book requires adequate preparation. As such, as an instructor, you should familiarize yourself with the content of the entire course, including its organization and approach. You should review each of the student activities and exercises so you can facilitate them in the classroom.

Throughout the book, you may see Instructor Notes that provide suggestions, answers to problems, and supplemental information for you, the instructor. You may also see references to "Additional Instructor Notes" that contain expanded instructional information; these notes appear in a separate section at the back of the book. PowerPoint slides may be provided on the included course files, which are available on the enclosed CD-ROM or by download from http://www.elementk.com/courseware-file-downloads. The slides are also referred to in the text. If you plan to use the slides, it is recommended to display them during the corresponding content as indicated in the instructor notes in the margin.

The course files may also include assessments for the course, which can be administered diagnostically before the class, or as a review after the course is completed. These exam-type questions can be used to gauge the students' understanding and assimilation of course content.

As a Review Tool

Any method of instruction is only as effective as the time and effort you, the student, are willing to invest in it. In addition, some of the information that you learn in class may not be important to you immediately, but it may become important later. For this reason, we encourage you to spend some time reviewing the content of the course after your time in the classroom.

As a Reference

The organization and layout of this book make it an easy-to-use resource for future reference. Taking advantage of the glossary, index, and table of contents, you can use this book as a first source of definitions, background information, and summaries.

Course Icons

Icon	Description
	A **Caution Note** makes students aware of potential negative consequences of an action, setting, or decision that are not easily known.
	Display Slide provides a prompt to the instructor to display a specific slide. Display Slides are included in the Instructor Guide only.
	An **Instructor Note** is a comment to the instructor regarding delivery, classroom strategy, classroom tools, exceptions, and other special considerations. Instructor Notes are included in the Instructor Guide only.
	Notes Page indicates a page that has been left intentionally blank for students to write on.
	A **Student Note** provides additional information, guidance, or hints about a topic or task.
	A **Version Note** indicates information necessary for a specific version of software.

Course Requirements and Setup

You can find a list of hardware and software requirements to run this class as well as detailed classroom setup procedures in the course files that are available on the CD-ROM that shipped with this book. If your course manual did not come with a CD-ROM, please go to **http://www.elementk.com/courseware-file-downloads** to download the files.

1 | Accessing PDF Documents

Lesson Time: 60 minutes

Lesson Objectives:

In this lesson, you will access information in a PDF document.

You will:

- Open a PDF document.
- Explore the Acrobat X Pro interface.
- Browse through a PDF document.

Introduction

You are likely to receive innumerable PDF documents with different types of information while at work. To read and make use of the information in a document, you must be able to access it. In this lesson, you will access information in PDF documents.

Working on an application without any prior knowledge of its interface will be a tedious task. Exploring the Adobe Acrobat application and understanding the functionality of its interface and components will enable you to access PDF documents and manage them effectively.

TOPIC A
Open PDF Documents

To access information in a document, you must be familiar with its file format. In this topic, you will access and open a PDF document.

Opening a PDF document enables you to display and view the contents of the document.

PDF

Portable Document Format (PDF) is the native file format for files accessed and modified using Adobe Acrobat. Using the **Print** command, you can convert any document in a particular format to a PDF document. The converted PDF document retains the appearance and print qualities of the original file, allowing the file to be accessed and printed independent of the file's native application and platform; minor changes and edits can be made in the PDF document.

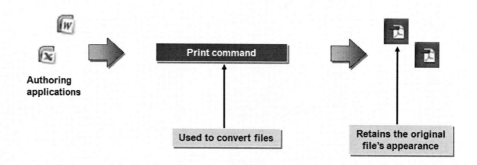

Figure 1-1: Conversion to a PDF document.

The Authoring Application

The *authoring application* is an application in which a file is originally created. PDF documents are created from existing documents created in other authoring applications. However, you cannot convert a PDF document to its native file format. Also, you cannot manipulate the content in a PDF document as you would do in the authoring application.

How to Open a PDF Document

Procedure Reference: Open a PDF Document

To open a PDF document:

1. Choose **Start→All Programs→Adobe Acrobat X Pro.**

2. Choose **File→Open.**

3. Navigate to the desired folder.

4. Open the desired file.

   - Select the file and click **Open.**

   - Double-click the desired file.

5. If necessary, choose **View→Read Mode** to maximize the viewing area and press **Esc** to return to the single-pane view.

6. If necessary, choose **View→Full Screen Mode** to fill the entire screen with the PDF page and press **Esc** to return to the single-pane view.

7. If necessary, choose **Window→Split** to view the document content in two panes and choose **Window→Remove Split** to return to the single-pane view.

8. If necessary, choose **Window→Spreadsheet Split** to view the document content in four panes and choose **Window→Remove Split** to return to the single-pane view.

ACTIVITY 1-1
Opening a PDF Document

Data Files:

C:\084548Data\Accessing PDF Documents\Employee Benefits.pdf

Scenario:

You work in the corporate office of Rudison Technologies. You received a PDF document on employee benefits. You want to view the contents of the document.

---

1. Open the PDF document and view its contents.

    a. Choose **Start→All Programs→Adobe Acrobat** X **Pro.**

    b. Choose **File→Open.**

    c. In the **Open** dialog box, navigate to the C:\084548Data\Accessing PDF Documents folder.

    d. Select the **Employee Benefits.pdf** file and click **Open** to open the document.

    e. Scroll down, and view the contents of the PDF document.

---

2. **Which command would you use to convert a document from any application to a PDF document?**

    a) The Save As command

    b) The Print command

    c) The Page Setup command

    d) The Print Preview command

TOPIC B
Explore the Adobe Acrobat X Pro Interface

You are asked to prepare a project report for your monthly presentation using Acrobat X Pro. To effectively work on a PDF document, you need to identify the use of its various components in the application window. In this topic, you will explore the Adobe Acrobat X Pro interface.

Building a strong foundation is crucial in understanding any subject. For example, unless a researcher conducts extensive research on his subject, it becomes difficult for him to complete his project. Similarly, before you begin working with Adobe Acrobat X Pro, you need to understand the basic features and functionality of the application. This would enable you to work with the application effectively.

The Welcome Screen

The Welcome Screen is displayed when the Acrobat X Pro application is launched. It has a number of sections that allow you to access recently opened files, open a file from the desired location, create PDF documents, and much more.

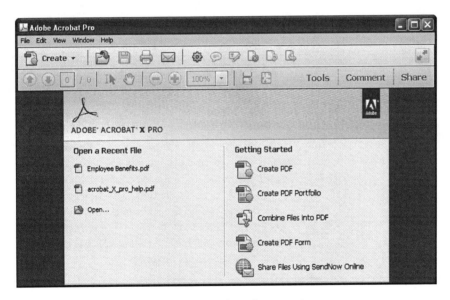

Figure 1-2: Overview of the Adobe Acrobat Pro Interface workspace.

Section	Allows You To
Open a Recent File	Open recently accessed files.
Create PDF	Convert a document created using any authoring application such as Microsoft Word, Adobe InDesign, Adobe FrameMaker, and so on. It also allows you to create PDF documents from a scanned document, a web page, a text document, or a digital photo.

Section	Allows You To
Create PDF Portfolio	Convert any document such as text documents, spreadsheets, email messages, CAD drawings, or PowerPoint presentations and assemble them in a single PDF portfolio unit.
Combine Files into PDF	Combine converted files into a compact PDF portfolio or a single PDF file.
Create PDF Form	Convert a PDF document, text document, or spreadsheet to PDF forms.
Share Files Using SendNow Online	Share documents on the web so that they are reviewed online using the Acrobat.com website.

The Adobe Acrobat Window

The *Adobe Acrobat* X *Pro window* has many interface elements that help you work with PDF documents.

Interface Element	Description
Menu bar	Provides access to menu commands.
Toolbars	Contains a set of buttons grouped based on their functionality.
Navigation Pane	Contains the navigation pane buttons such as **Articles, Attachments, Bookmarks, Content, Destinations, Layers, Model Tree, Order, Page Thumbnails, Signatures,** and **Tags.** Each button when clicked displays a list of elements in its associated panel.
Document pane	Displays the content of the PDF documents.
Task pane	Contains the **Tools, Comment,** and **Share** panels. The **Tools** panel consists of various tools for tasks ranging from page manipulation to form creation, text recognition, securing documents, and digital signatures. The **Comment** panel has various options that can be used to mark up or add comments to a PDF document. The **Share** panel makes it easy to share files on the Acrobat.com website, an online file sharing service, or to send them as attachments or links.

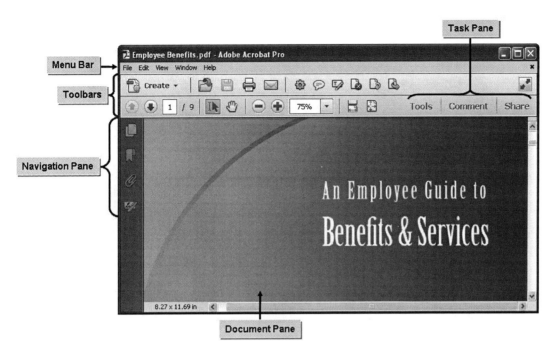

Figure 1-3: Components of the Adobe Acrobat X Pro Interface window.

Adobe Acrobat X Pro Help

The **Adobe Acrobat X Pro Help** command is available on the **Help** menu in the Adobe Acrobat X Pro window. It enables you to search for help topics in a separate window.

Adobe Acrobat and Adobe Reader

Adobe Acrobat is used to create PDF files, whereas Adobe Reader is used to view them. Adobe Reader is a freeware and is downloadable from Adobe's website.

Toolbars

There are different toolbars available in Acrobat. Toolbars make the work area less cluttered by arranging the tools in task-related groups.

Figure 1-4: Toolbars in the Adobe Acrobat X Pro Interface.

Toolbar	Description
Create	A drop-down menu that can be used to create PDF documents from files, scanned documents, web pages, forms, and portfolios. This drop-down menu can also be used to combine PDFs from other source of files, folders, clipboards, scanned documents, and email messages.
Quick Tools	A set of tools that can be used to edit and modify a PDF document.
Common Tools	A set of tools that can be used to perform the most common tasks in a PDF document.
Page Navigation	An interface element that can be used to navigate through the pages of a PDF document.
Select & Zoom	A tool that can be used to select text and images and to magnify PDF documents.
Page Display	Used to scroll down and view the page in one or more layouts.

The Grabber Bar

Each toolbar has a grabber bar, which is a vertical gray stripe at the left end of the toolbar. It can be used to drag the associated toolbar to a different location.

Streamlined User Interface

Adobe Acrobat X Pro is designed as a user-friendly interface for easily locating and accessing tools. The Task pane contains the most commonly used tools that help you locate, view, edit, and organize information in a PDF document.

How to Explore the Adobe Acrobat X Pro Interface

Procedure Reference: Explore the Acrobat X Pro Interface

To explore the Acrobat X Pro interface:

1. Launch the Adobe Acrobat X Pro application.

2. Open the desired file.

3. Explore the interface.

   ● Click a menu to view its commands and choose a menu command to view its submenus.

   ● On the Common Tools toolbar, position the mouse pointer on a button to view the tooltip.

   ● Right-click the desired toolbar to view the context menu.

   ● In the **Navigation Pane,** click the desired panel button to display the associated panel and then click the **Collapse** button to collapse the panel.

   ● On the Common Tools toolbar, click the page navigation buttons to navigate within the document.

   ● Explore the options on the **Quick Tools** toolbar.

   ● On the Common Tools toolbar, click the select and zoom buttons to zoom in on or zoom out the selected text or image in the document.

Procedure Reference: Customize the Toolbars

To customize the toolbars:

1. Open the Acrobat X Pro application.

2. If necessary, choose **View→Show/HideView→Toolbar Items** to hide or display the available tools.

 The check mark next to the toolbar name indicates that the toolbar is displayed.

3. Customize the toolbars.

   ● Drag the grabber bar of a tool to reposition the tool in the **Quick Tools** toolbar section.

   ● In the appropriate panel, right-click the desired button and choose **Add to Quick Tools** to add tools to the toolbar.

   ● Using the **Customize Quick Tools** dialog box, add tools to the **Quick Tools** toolbar.

      a. On the Common Tools toolbar, click the **Customize Quick Tools** button.

      b. In the **Customize Quick Tools** dialog box, in the **Choose Quick Tools To Add** section, expand the desired panels.

      c. In the left pane, select any toolbar options and click the Right Arrow button to add tools to the **Quick Tools** toolbar.

      d. If necessary, in the **Quick Tools To Show** section, select any of desired listed toolbar option and click the Left Arrow button to remove the tool from the toolbar.

      e.   If necessary, to change the position of a tool, click the Up or Down Arrow button.

      f.   If necessary, to add a vertical line to separate the tools in a group, click the Separator button.

      g.   Click **OK** to close the **Customize Quick Tools** dialog box.

- Drag the grabber bar of a toolbar from one position to another within the toolbar area to rearrange the docked toolbars.

4.   If necessary, reset the settings.

- Choose **View→Show/Hide→Toolbars Items→Reset Toolbars** to reset all the toolbars to their default settings.

- Choose **View→Show/Hide→Navigation Panes→Reset Panes** to restore all the navigation panels to their default settings.

ACTIVITY 1-2

Exploring the Adobe Acrobat X Pro Interface

Before You Begin:

The Employee Benefits.pdf file is open.

Scenario:

Your manager has requested you to assist in preparing a project report. You have to prepare a document using the Acrobat application. Because you do not have any prior hands-on experience with the application, you would like to get yourself acquainted with its components and you want to understand its functions that it might be easy to use them on the job.

---

1. Explore the menu commands.

    a. Choose **File→Create.**

    b. Observe the commands on the **Create** submenu.

    c. Click **File** to hide the menu.

    d. Choose **View→Tools.**

    e. Observe the commands on the **Tools** submenu.

    f. Click **View** to hide the menu.

    g. Similarly, explore the other menus and view the commands.

---

2. Explore the options on the toolbar.

    a. On the Quick Tools toolbar, position the mouse pointer on the **Customize Quick Tools** button [icon] to view the tooltip.

    b. On the Quick Tools toolbar, in the blank space, right-click to display the various commands.

    c. Position the mouse pointer over the **Page Navigation** command to view a menu of page navigation commands.

    d. Click the Quick Tools toolbar to hide the menu.

    e. Similarly, view the expanded menu for each toolbar.

---

3. Explore the **Navigation Pane.**

    a. Select the **Tools** panel and expand the **Pages** section.

    b. Observe the various options in the **Pages** section.

    c. In the **Navigation Pane,** click the **Page Thumbnails** button. [icon]

    d. Observe that the **Page Thumbnails** panel is displayed.

    e. In the **Navigation Pane,** click the Bookmarks button. [icon]

---

f.   Observe that the **Bookmarks** panel is displayed.

g.   Similarly, navigate to and observe the panels displayed by clicking the buttons in the **Navigation Pane.**

TOPIC C
Browse Through PDF Documents

You identified the components of the Acrobat interface. You may now want to access the information displayed in the multi-page PDF documents. In this topic, you will browse through the pages of a PDF document.

Browsing through a PDF document enables you to read and review the information in it. Also, Acrobat provides options that enable you to magnify the contents in a PDF document so that reading is comfortable on screen.

PDF Page Layout Views

Adobe Acrobat X Pro provides you with four page layout views to view a PDF document.

Page Layout View	*Description*
Single Page View	Displays one page at a time, regardless of the magnification size.
Enable Scrolling	Enables scrolling of pages in a PDF document with the pages stacked vertically. When you scroll to the bottom of a page, the next page is displayed below in a single-page view.
Two Page View	Displays facing pages as a spread. A spread is a pair of pages facing one another such as in books and magazines. In this view, a document's first page appears by itself on the right side, much like a book cover or a chapter page that appears on the right side in a printed book.
Two Page Scrolling	Displays a pair of facing pages with the spreads stacked vertically. When you scroll to the bottom of one spread, the next spread is displayed below.
Show Gaps Between Pages	Displays gaps between pages.
Show Cover Page in Two Page View	Displays the cover page of the document as a spread so that the cover page appears on the right side as in a printed book.
Automatically Scroll	Enables automatic scrolling of the pages in a PDF document at a steady rate, with the pages stacked vertically. When you interrupt the scrolling process and manually adjust the scroll bars for navigating forward or backward, automatic scrolling continues from that point of navigation. At the end of the document, automatic scrolling stops until you enable automatic scrolling again.

Using the Zoom Components

There are several components to adjust the magnification in a particular PDF document. These components are available on the **Select & Zoom** toolbar.

Component	Result
Marquee Zoom button	Magnifies a specific area of the page selected using this tool. When you click the document after selecting the tool, it enlarges the entire page.
Dynamic Zoom button	Continuously increases the magnification of the selected text or image when the mouse button is rolled forward and continuously decreases the magnification of the selected text or image when the mouse button is rolled back.
Zoom Out button	Minimizes the view of the document according to the zoom percentage specified.
Zoom In button	Maximizes the view of the document according to the zoom percentage specified.
Zoom Value text box	Displays the PDF at the magnification you specify.
Actual Size button	Displays the PDF page at 100 percent magnification.
Zoom to Page Level button	Lets you change the magnification of the PDF so that the page appears vertical in the document pane.
Fit Width button	Displays the current PDF page or spread so that its width matches that of the window.
Pan & Zoom window	Lets you use a small window to adjust the magnification and position of the view area, similar to using a page thumbnail.
Loupe tool	Lets you view a magnified portion of the document in an adjustable rectangle in the document pane. This tool is especially useful for zooming in to see fine details in PDF documents.
Snapshot tool	Captures a selection as an image. Both text and images within the selection are stored as an image in the clipboard. This content can be pasted into another application.
Fit Height button	Displays the current PDF page or spread so that it fits the height of the window.
Fit Visible button	Displays the current PDF page or spread, so that its text and images fits the width of the window.

Resize Pages

Using the **Zoom** tool, the document pages can be resized to fit entirely in the document pane, to fit to the width of the window, to fit to the height of the window, and to partly fit so that only the text and images are visible, and the other part of the page is out of view.

Page Navigation Options

Using the options on the **Page Navigation** toolbar, you can navigate to any page, first page, previous page, next page, last page, and also view the new and original version of the document with changes.

The Read Mode

The *Read mode* is a feature that helps you get the maximum view of a document. In this mode, the toolbars, the Task pane, and the navigation panes are all hidden, and a floating bar appears at the bottom of the window with navigation controls. These navigation controls can be used to navigate to the previous page, to the next page, or to any page in the document.

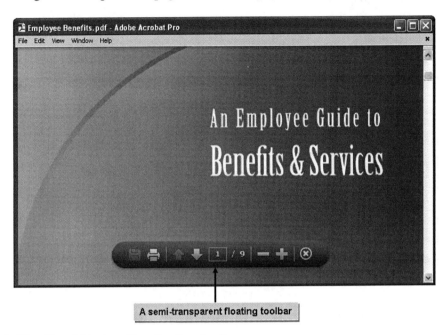

Figure 1-5: The Read Mode with a floating toolbar.

Floating Toolbars

When you choose to view the document in the Read mode, a semi-transparent toolbar with basic navigation and zoom controls appears near the bottom of the window. The toolbar can be moved to the desired location in the window. Using the options in the toolbar, you can save and print a file, zoom in or zoom out, or navigate to the previous page, next page, or to any page in the document.

The Full Screen Mode

The *Full Screen* mode is a mode that is used to view the document page on the entire screen, similar to an online presentation. You can set preferences for PDF documents to open in the Full Screen mode so as to enable a consistent view of the document. You can also add page transitions to enhance the visual effect of the document.

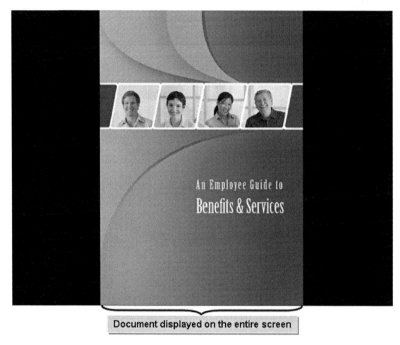

Figure 1-6: Presentation of a PDF document in full screen.

How to Browse Through a PDF Document
Procedure Reference: Browse Through a PDF Document

To browse through a PDF document:

1. Choose **View→Page Display** and then choose the desired command to set the page lay-out.
2. Navigate through the pages.
   - Scroll down a page to view the content on the next page.
   - On the **Page Navigation** toolbar, click the **Previous Page** or **Next Page** button to navigate to the desired page, or type the number of the page you want to view in the given text box and press **Enter.**
   - Choose **View→Page Navigation** and then choose the **First Page, Previous Page, Next Page, Last Page,** or **Page** command to navigate to the desired page.
   - In the **Navigation Pane,** click the **Page Thumbnails** button and click a page's thumbnail to navigate to that page.
3. If necessary, change the current page magnification.
   a. Choose **View→Zoom→Zoom To.**
   b. In the **Zoom To** dialog box, set the zoom value.
      - In the **Magnification** text box, type the desired zoom value and press **OK.**
      - From the **Magnification** drop-down list, select a preset zoom value and click **OK.**
4. If necessary, move to the previous view.
   - Choose **View→Page Navigation→Previous View** or;
   - Press **Alt+Left Arrow.**

5.   If necessary, move to the next view.

    ●   Choose **View→Page Navigation→Next View** or;

    ●   Press **Alt+Right Arrow.**

6.   Click the **Close** button to close the PDF document.

ACTIVITY 1-3
Browsing Through a PDF Document

Before you Begin:
The Employee Benefits.pdf is open.

Scenario:
You received the Employee Benefits guide for this quarter end. You would like to browse through the Employee Benefits guide to see if it contains any news that might be of interest to you. But first, you are curious to see if the Employee Benefits guide contains any photographs of people you know.

---

1. Navigate to few of the pages containing images.

   a. In the **Navigation Pane,** click the **Page Thumbnails** button to display the **Page Thumbnail** panel.

   b. Select the page 3 thumbnail to view the contents of the page in the document pane.

   c. In the **Page Thumbnails** panel, scroll down and select the page 5 thumbnail.

---

2. Display the Employee Benefits guide so that you have a full view of each page spread in the document window.

   a. Choose **View→Zoom→Zoom To.**

   b. In the **Zoom To** dialog box, in the **Magnification** drop-down list, scroll up and select **Fit Page** to fit the entire page in the document window and click **OK.**

   c. Choose **View→Page Display→Two Page View** to have a full view of each page spread.

---

3. Browse through the content in the Employee Benefits guide.

   a. In the **Page Thumbnails** panel, scroll up and select the page 1 thumbnail.

   b. On the **Page Navigation** toolbar, click the **Show next page** button, 🔽 to display pages 3 and 4 side by side.

   c. Navigate to each additional page spread until you reach the end of the document.

   d. Choose **View→Page Navigation→Previous View** to return to the previous view.

   e. Choose **File→Close** to close the document.

---

4. **Which toolbar contains the tools to browse through a PDF document?**

   a) The Tasks toolbar

   b) The Select & Zoom toolbar

   c) The Page Navigation toolbar

   d) The Page Display toolbar

Lesson 1 Follow-up

In this lesson, you accessed a PDF document and browsed through its content. This will enable you to access the information in the document with ease.

1. **Which navigation technique will be useful for your work? Why?**

2. **How does exploring the interface help you to make use of the Acrobat application at work? Discuss.**

2 | Creating PDF Documents

Lesson Time: 1 hour(s), 35 minutes

Lesson Objectives:

In this lesson, you will create PDF documents.

You will:

- Create a PDF document from a file.
- Create a PDF document using the Print command.
- Create a PDF document from web pages.
- Create a PDF document using email applications.
- Create a PDF document using Acrobat.

Introduction

Information available in PDF documents can be easily accessed and reused by everyone. Now, you may want to send information to others in a format they can easily access. In this lesson, you will convert documents in other formats to a PDF document.

The ability to convert any file into a universally accepted format enables you to share documents with a wider group of audience. Using Acrobat, you can convert any file into PDF and reuse the contents of a file without any modification.

TOPIC A
Create PDF Documents from a File

You accessed a PDF document that contains information. Sometimes, lots of information will be available to you in formats other than a PDF document, and you may want to access them. In this topic, you will convert Microsoft Office documents or documents of other formats to PDF documents.

Saving a Microsoft Office document or document in a different file format may compromise the document's layout and appearance. Using Acrobat to convert the documents, you can generate a PDF version of the document, while retaining the document's original font, layout, and formatting.

The Create Drop-Down Menu

The **Create** drop-down menu allows you to generate PDF documents from files created using other applications or scanners, or from web pages.

Options	Used To
PDF from File	Generate a PDF of a file created in different applications such as Microsoft Word, Microsoft Excel, Microsoft PowerPoint, Wordpad, or Notepad. This helps retain the font, formatting, and layout of the original document.
PDF from Scanner	Create a PDF file from scanned pages. You can configure settings and customize output as required.
Create PDF from Web Page	Generate a PDF file of web pages with links so that they can be accessed offline.
PDF from Clipboard	Create a PDF file by copying the text from any source.
Combine Files into a Single PDF	Combine multiple PDF files into a single PDF file. You can add or exclude files according to the requirement. You can also order files in the sequence you need.
PDF Form	Create static or interactive PDF forms. You can create forms for files that are already open in the Acrobat X Pro interface or from a scanned paper form. You can also import files that have form fields. This allows you to include the information or details about participants in activities such as a survey or a review or any other task that requires data about the stakeholders.
PDF Portfolio	Combine multiple PDF documents or files of other formats into a single portfolio or unit retaining the file in the original format. This may be used in cases where the information is available in different formats.

Portfolios

A portfolio is a PDF document that is created by combining PDF documents and may also include documents of other formats. The **PDF Portfolio** option is used to collate files such as text documents, Microsoft Office files, email messages, or even CAD drawings into a single PDF file, while allowing you to edit the documents separately in the Portfolio pane.

How to Create a PDF Document from a File

Procedure Reference: Specify Adobe PDF Conversion Settings

To specify the Adobe PDF conversion settings:

1. In the Microsoft Word application, on the **Acrobat** tab, in the **Create PDF** group, click **Preferences.**

2. If necessary, in the **Acrobat PDFMaker** dialog box, select the **Settings** tab.

3. From the **Conversion Settings** drop-down list, select the desired Adobe PDF preset.

4. If necessary, click **Advanced Settings** and customize the PDF settings to meet the preferred output requirement.

    a. In the left pane, select a folder and specify the settings in the right pane.

    b. Click **Save As** to save the customized PDF setting for later use or reuse.

    c. If necessary, rename the file.

    d. Click **OK** to close the **[Adobe Preset](number) - Adobe PDF Settings** dialog box.

5. If necessary, select the **Security** tab and set a password that a user must enter to open the file.

6. If necessary, use the **Word** tab, and convert comments to notes, footnote and endnote links, and enable the advanced tagging feature.

7. If necessary, select the **Bookmarks** tab and in the **Bookmark Options** section, check the desired check boxes.

8. In the **Acrobat PDFMaker** dialog box, click **OK** to apply the PDF conversion settings.

The Acrobat PDFMaker Dialog Box

The **Acrobat PDFMaker** dialog box consists of two tabs that help you convert a file from a PDFMaker-enabled application to a PDF file. You can display this dialog box in Microsoft Word by clicking the **Preferences** button in the **Create Adobe PDF** group of the **Acrobat** tab.

Tab	Allows You To
Settings	Specify the conversion settings for PDFMaker. This tab also includes the **Advanced Settings** button that allows you to specify a file name for the new print preset. You can also specify settings for items including fonts, colors, images, and other file options.
Security	Specify the security setting such as a password or include permissions to edit the PDF document. You can also specify the settings for encryptions.

 The options in the **PDFMaker Settings** and **Application Settings** sections in the **Acrobat PDFMaker** dialog box vary according to the file type you choose. At any time, you can restore the dialog box to the default settings by clicking the **Restore Defaults** button at the bottom of the dialog box.

Adobe PDF Conversion Settings

The *Acrobat PDFMaker conversion settings* determine the characteristics of the PDF files you generate.

Conversion Setting	Description
High Quality Print	Creates PDF files for high-quality printing and embeds subsets of all fonts.
Oversized Pages	Creates PDF files that can display and print engineering drawings larger than 200 x 200 inches.
PDF/A-1b:2005 (CMYK)	Creates PDF files using PDF 1.4 compatibility settings, and converts all colors used in the document to CMYK.
PDF/A-1b:2005 (RGB)	Creates PDF files using PDF 1.4 compatibility settings, and converts all colors used in the document to RGB.
PDF/X-1a:2001	Creates PDF files that are compliant with PDF/X-1a:2001, an ISO standard for graphic content exchange.
PDF/X-3:2002	Creates PDF files that are compliant with PDF/X-3:2002, an ISO standard for graphic content exchange.
Press Quality	Creates PDF files for professional print production. The **Press Quality** setting generates files similar to files generated by the **High Quality Print** setting, embedding the required fonts. This ensures that the fonts appear as intended.
Smallest File Size	Creates PDF files for online distribution and on-screen viewing as it generates small files for fast downloads. It may not produce sufficient quality graphics for printing as it creates PDFs with low image resolution.
Standard	Creates PDF files with a reasonable balance between the file size and the printing quality for most business needs, such as printing from desktop printers or distributing through CD-ROM.

PDF Creation in Windows 7 and Office 2010 Applications

You can create PDF documents from within the Microsoft Office 2010 applications using the **Acrobat PDFMaker** dialog box. The Microsoft Windows 7 operating system also supports creation of PDF documents. While converting PDF documents from Microsoft Word, PowerPoint, or Excel, you can define the conversion settings for the file. You can also select specific content in the file and convert that into a PDF document. However, any changes you make to the conversion settings apply only to the specific documents. The **Acrobat PDFMaker** dialog box has an option that allows you to embed multimedia files in Microsoft Word and PowerPoint files. These multimedia files are converted to the FLV format that will be played once the Microsoft Word and PowerPoint files are converted to the PDF format. You can also convert files created using applications such as Microsoft Project or Visio to PDF files.

PDF 1.4 Compatibility Settings

PDF 1.4 is a PDF compatibility setting that opens a PDF file using Acrobat and Reader versions 6.0 or above. Version 1.4 was the basis for the chief versions of ISO standards PDF/X and PDF/A. PDF/X is a middle-level setting used to send images to printers. This ensures that the PDF is compatible with earlier versions of the software. This is also referred to as Acrobat 5.0 (PDF 1.4) compatibility setting.

Font Embedding and Substitution

A font is embedded into a PDF document when the source document is converted into a PDF file using the authoring tool. The font that has to be embedded in a PDF document can be mentioned in the **Standard - Adobe PDF Settings** dialog box in an authoring application such as Microsoft Word. The fonts that you add from the **Always Embed** list box of the **Embedding** section are embedded in the generated PDF file. Embedding prevents font substitution when readers view or print the file and ensures that they see the text in its original font. Embedding increases the file size if the document uses double-byte fonts (a font format commonly used for Asian languages).

Procedure Reference: Create a PDF Document Using Microsoft Office Applications

To create a PDF document using Microsoft Office applications:

1. Open the Microsoft Word or Excel document you want to convert to PDF.
2. Display the **Save Adobe PDF File As** dialog box.
   - Select the **Acrobat** tab and in the **Create Adobe PDF** group, click **Create PDF** or;
   - Choose **File→Save as Adobe PDF**.
3. Select the **Acrobat** tab and in the **Create Adobe PDF** group, click **Create PDF.**
4. Navigate to the folder where you want to save the file.
5. In the **File name** text box, type a file name and click **Save.**

 The PDFMaker support for Microsoft Office 2000 is unavailable. Acrobat X Pro is not compatible with Microsoft Office 2000. Also, Acrobat X Pro PDFMaker is not available for Mac OS.

Fit Worksheet to Single Page

The Fit worksheet to single page is a printer setting that needs to be applied before converting an Excel sheet into a PDF document so that the entire worksheet fits within the width of a PDF page. The **Fit Sheet on One Page** option available on the **No Scaling** drop-down menu of the **Settings** section can be used to specify this setting.

Adobe PDF Compatibility Settings

Before setting the advanced settings in the **Acrobat PDFMaker** dialog box for creating a PDF, you can specify the compatibility settings of the document. By specifying the compatibility settings, you can determine the audience who would have access to the document. Selecting the most recent version from the **Compatibility** drop-down list will enable you to include the latest features in the document. Whereas, selecting an older version of compatibility will enable you to distribute the document to a larger audience who do not have the latest version of the software.

Procedure Reference: Create a PDF Document from a Copied Selection

To create a PDF document from a copied selection:

1.   Copy the desired content.
2.   Open the Acrobat application.
3.   Choose **Create→PDF From Clipboard.**
4.   If necessary, choose **File→Save,** specify the file name, and click **OK** to save the document.

Procedure Reference: Create a PDF Document from a Selected Content

To create a PDF document from a selected content:

1.   Select the content from the desired application.
2.   Open the desired Microsoft Office document.
3.   Select the **Acrobat** tab and in the **Create Adobe PDF** group, click the **Create PDF** button.
4.   In the **Save Adobe PDF File As** dialog box, click **Options.**
5.   In the **Page range** section, select the **Selection** option and click **OK.**
6.   If necessary, in the **Save Adobe PDF File As** dialog box, rename the file and click **Save.**

ACTIVITY 2-1
Converting a Microsoft Office Word Document to PDF

Data Files:

C:\084548Data\Creating PDF Documents\Employee Benefits.docx

Before You Begin:

1. Choose **Start→All Programs→Microsoft Office→Microsoft Word 2010** to open the Microsoft Office Word 2010 application.

2. From the C:\084548Data\Creating PDF Documents folder, open the Employee Benefits.docx file.

Scenario:

You made some changes to the Employee Wellness section of the Employee Benefits guide. You want to send a read-only copy of the updated document to the employees in such a way that the original formatting of the content is retained, and the document can be printed at a reasonable quality.

---

1. Specify the PDF conversion settings for the document.

   a. Select the **Acrobat** tab and in the **Create Adobe PDF** group, click **Preferences.**

   b. In the **Acrobat PDFMaker** dialog box, in the **PDFMaker Settings** section, in the **Conversion Settings** drop-down list, verify that **Standard** is selected.

   c. Click **Advanced Settings.**

   d. In the **Standard - Adobe PDF Settings** dialog box, in the **File Options** section, from the **Compatibility** drop-down list, select **Acrobat 5.0 (PDF 1.4).**

   e. In the left pane, select the **Images** category.

   f. In the right pane, in the **Color Images** section, in the first **pixels per inch** text box, verify that **150** is displayed.

   g. Click **Save As** to display the **Save Adobe PDF Settings As** dialog box.

   h. In the **File name** text box, type *Desktop Print* and click **Save** to save the customized preset.

   i. In the **Desktop Print - Adobe PDF Settings** dialog box, click **OK.**

   j. In the **Acrobat PDFMaker** dialog box, click **OK** to save the customized preset titled "Desktop Print" for reuse.

---

2. Convert the Employee Wellness page of the Employee Benefits.docx document to a PDF document.

   a. Scroll down to the Employee Wellness page of the document and at the top-left corner of the image, click before the image.

   b. Scroll down the page, hold down **Shift,** and click after the text "rudisontechnologies.com" (after the period) to select the entire page.

---

c. On the **Acrobat** tab, in the **Create Adobe PDF** group, click **Create PDF.**

d. In the **Save Adobe PDF File As** dialog box, click **Options.**

e. In the **Acrobat PDFMaker** dialog box, in the **Page range** section, select the **Selection** option and click **OK.**

f. If necessary, in the **Save Adobe PDF File As** dialog box, navigate to the C:\084548Data\Creating PDF Documents folder.

g. In the **File name** text box, click and type *Employee Wellness*

h. Click **Save** to save the PDF file.

 The conversion of the Microsoft Word document to a PDF could take some time.

i. View the contents of the Employee Wellness.pdf file.

j. Close the Employee Wellness.pdf file.

k. Switch to the Microsoft Word application.

l. Select the **File** tab and choose **Exit** to close the Microsoft Word application.

TOPIC B

Create a PDF Document Using the Print Command

You generated PDF documents from files created using other applications. Another way to create a PDF version of a document is by using the **Print** command in the authoring application. In this topic, you will generate the PDF of a document by specifying options in the authoring application's **Print** dialog box.

Some applications such as Microsoft Word and Adobe InDesign provide specific commands for creating PDF versions of existing documents, but there are other applications that do not have such commands. Even if an application does not provide specific PDF conversion options, you can still generate PDF documents from the application using its **Print** command.

The Adobe PDF Printer

In authoring applications that do not support PDF conversion, you can use the Adobe PDF printer to convert a file to a PDF document. The default printing preferences apply to all applications that use the Adobe PDF printer. You can change the printing preference settings in an authoring application.

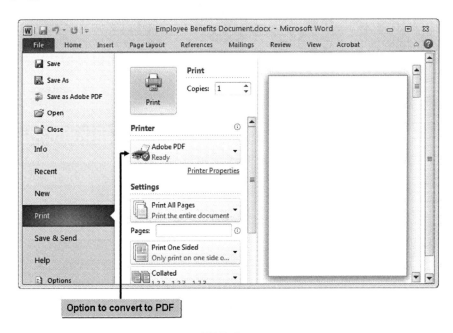

Figure 2-1: Print options to convert to a PDF document.

Generating PDFs for Electronic Distribution

Creating a PDF using the **Print** dialog box will not add navigation aids to the PDF file; so, you should use an application-specific method for generating PDF documents, if the document should include elements such as links, articles, or bookmarks. However, some applications such as Adobe Illustrator and Photoshop create only single-page files and do not add links to PDF files when you use their built-in PDF generation commands. The **Print** dialog box is equally valid for electronic distribution in such instances.

How to Create a PDF Document Using the Print Command

Procedure Reference: Create a PDF Document Using the Print Command

To create a PDF document using the **Print** command:

1. Open the file in its authoring application.

2. Choose **File→Print** to display the application's print options.

3. In the **Printer** section, from the drop-down list, select **Adobe PDF.**

4. If necessary, click the **Printer Properties** link to display the **Document Properties** dialog box, specify the required Adobe PDF printer settings, and click **OK.**

5. Click **Print.**

6. In the **Save PDF File As** dialog box, navigate to the desired location to save the file.

7. In the **File name** text box, type a file name for the PDF document and click **Save** to display the generated PDF.

Adobe PDF Printing Preferences

The settings you specify in the **Adobe PDF Printing Preferences** dialog box will be used as default by other applications unless you define different settings from within an application. You can select a predefined Adobe PDF setting and a security option, specify the location to store the converted PDF file and the page size, and include document information such as the source document's file name and creation date in this dialog box. It also contains other options that will allow you to speed up PDF creation, open the converted PDF in Acrobat, automatically delete the log file generated, and prevent the PDF file you create from overwriting an existing file that has the same name.

ACTIVITY 2-2
Converting to PDF Using a Printer

Data Files:

C:\084548Data\Creating PDF Documents\Staff Contacts.xlsx

Before You Begin:

1. Choose **Start→All Programs→Microsoft Office→Microsoft Excel 2010 to open the Microsoft Office Excel 2010** application.

2. From the C:\084548Data\Creating PDF Documents folder, open the Staff Contacts.xlsx file.

Scenario:

Several employees in your office have requested a list of office phone extensions and residence numbers of all employees. This list is available to you in the Microsoft Excel format. However, not all employees have the Microsoft Office suite. You decide to convert the Excel sheet into a PDF and circulate it among the employees. You delegate this responsibility to one of your subordinates who does not have Acrobat X Pro installed on his system.

---

1. Specify the print settings necessary for generating a PDF.

   a. Select the **File** tab and choose **Print.**

   b. In the **Printer** section, in the drop-down list, verify that **Adobe PDF** is selected.

   c. In the **Printer** section, click the **Printer Properties** link.

   d. In the **Adobe PDF Document Properties** dialog box, in the **Adobe PDF Conversion Settings** section, in the **Default Settings** drop-down list, verify that **Standard** is selected.

---

2. Generate the PDF document.

   a. Verify that the **View Adobe PDF results** check box is checked and click **OK.**

   b. In the **Print** section, click **Print.**

   c. In the **Save PDF File As** dialog box, navigate to the C:\084548Data\Creating PDF Documents folder.

   d. Click **Save.**

   e. Observe that the Staff Contacts.xlsx file is converted to a PDF document. Close the Staff Contacts.pdf file.

   f. Switch to the Microsoft Excel application.

   g. Select the **File** tab and choose **Exit** to close the Microsoft Excel application.

TOPIC C
Create a PDF Document from Web Pages

You created PDF documents using the **Print** command. As part of your job requirement, you may have to capture web pages and store them for future offline reference. Acrobat X Pro gives you the option to convert an entire website or a single web page or part of a web page to a PDF document. In this topic, you will convert web pages into PDF documents.

While browsing through the Internet, you find many websites containing tips on using software applications. However, the sites may provide only online content, which requires you to be connected to the Internet to view the content. You may want to use the content as reference material offline. By creating PDF documents of websites or web pages with Acrobat, you need not be connected to the Internet all the time to view a web page or use online content.

The Advanced Selection Feature

The Advanced selection feature allows you to select a part of the web page that you would like to convert to a PDF document. You can enable the Advanced selection feature by clicking the **Select** button on the **Adobe PDF** toolbar. You can then use the **Convert** option to convert the selection to a PDF document.

 When you install Acrobat X Pro, the **Adobe PDF** toolbar is added to Internet Explorer. You can select the buttons on the **Adobe PDF** toolbar to convert web pages to PDF.

The Internet Explorer - Adobe PDF Toolbar

When you install Acrobat X Pro, the **Adobe PDF** toolbar is added to Internet Explorer. You can use the elements on the **Adobe PDF** toolbar, located below the Address bar, to convert web pages to PDF.

Mozilla Firefox Support

You can convert web pages displayed using the Mozilla Firefox browser to PDF documents maintaining the links. You can also add a web page to a PDF file or convert a web page to PDF and email it. You can convert a web page and print it by choosing the **Print Web Page** command from the **Convert** drop-down menu. You can use the **Preferences** command to specify conversion settings, PDF settings, and page layout settings.

How to Create a PDF Document from Web Pages

Procedure Reference: Convert Web Pages to a PDF Document Using Acrobat

To convert web pages to a PDF document using Acrobat:

1. In the Acrobat X Pro application, choose **File→Create PDF→From Web Page.**

2. In the **Create PDF from Web Page** dialog box, specify the website or page you want to convert.

    *   In the **URL** text box, type the address of the website or;

    *   Click **Browse** and in the **Select File to Open** dialog box, navigate to and select the desired website and then click **Select.**

3. Click the **Capture Multiple Levels** button and in the **Settings** section, specify the desired settings.

    *   Select **Get entire site** to convert the entire site to PDF.

    *   Select **Get only** and then type a number in the **Levels** text box to indicate the number of site levels you want to include in the PDF.

    *   Check the **Stay on same path** check box to include the web pages that are subordinate to the one you selected in the **URL** text box.

    *   Check the **Stay on same server** check box to include the web pages that are stored on the same server as the page you selected in the **URL** text box.

4. If necessary, click **Settings** to specify additional settings for controlling the conversion of web content and then click **OK.**

5. In the **Create PDF from Web Page** dialog box, click **Create** to create the PDF document.

6. In the **Potentially Large Download Confirmation** message box, click **Yes** to create the PDF document.

7. Save the generated PDF in the preferred location with the appropriate file name.

8. If necessary, in the generated PDF, click the links to navigate to the related web pages.

 If you right-click a link to a resource that was not converted as part of the PDF, four commands are displayed. If you want to open the resource link in a web browser, choose **Open Weblink in Browser.** If you want to open the link in Acrobat, choose **Append to Document** to add it to the end of the current PDF document. If you want to open the link as a new document in Acrobat, choose **Open Weblink as New Document.** If you want to copy the link location, you can choose **Copy Link Location.**

Procedure Reference: Convert Specific Web Content to a PDF Document

To convert specific web content to a PDF document:

1. Open a web page.

2. Select the content to be converted.

    *   Click at the beginning of the content, hold down **Shift,** and click at the end of the content or;

    *   Click and drag to select the content or;

    *   On the **Adobe PDF** toolbar, click **Select** to enable the **Advanced selection** feature and then select the part of the web page you want to convert into a PDF.

3. Convert the selected content into a PDF document.
   - Right-click the selection and choose the desired command or;
   - From the **Convert** drop-down menu, choose the desired command.
4. In the **Convert Web Page to Adobe PDF** dialog box, navigate to the location to save the PDF file.
5. In the **File name** text box, specify a name.
6. Click **Save** to save the PDF document.

Improved Output Fidelity of HTML to PDF Conversion

Files written in HTML form a significant part of web pages. The HTML files are associated with other files that determine the way a web page works. When you convert a web page to a PDF, the HTML file and all the associated files such as JPEG and Bitmap images, cascading style sheets, Javascript pages and so on are included in the conversion process and the PDF looks similar to the original web page.

Convert Web Page Selections to PDF

You can determine whether to convert just the selection made within a web page to a PDF file, or convert the target page of the links in the selection, if any, as part of the PDF. The conversion commands on the shortcut menu vary depending on the content on which you right-click.

Option	*Description*
Append Link Target to Existing PDF	The link's target page is appended to the currently open PDF document.
Append to Existing PDF	The selected content is appended to the currently open PDF.
Convert Link Target to Adobe PDF	The link's target page is converted to a new PDF document.
Convert to Adobe PDF	The selection is converted to a new PDF. If the selection is a graphic link, only the individual link is converted into a PDF. Whereas, the entire web page gets converted if you select any one of the text links for conversion. When you click the links from within the PDF document, the target pages of the links are displayed.

ACTIVITY 2-3
Converting a Website to PDF

Before You Begin:

The Adobe Acrobat X Pro application is open.

Scenario:

You work in the marketing division of one of the leading web portals dedicated to coffee lovers. The new website is ready, and you want to get feedback on the website from your colleagues. However, not all of them may have an Internet connection. So, you decide to convert the website to a PDF document in order to enable other staff members to review it offline.

1. Convert all pages on the Everything For Coffee website to a single PDF document.

    a. In the Acrobat X Pro application, choose **File→Create→PDF from Web Page.**

    b. In the **Create PDF from Web Page** dialog box, in the **URL** text box, type *www.everythingforcoffee.com*

    c. Click the **Capture Multiple Levels** button.

    d. In the **Settings** section, select the **Get entire site** option and click **Create.**

    e. In the **Potentially Large Download Confirmation** message box, click **Yes** to create the PDF document.

    f. Observe that the website is converted to a PDF document and displayed in a new window.

     The conversion of the web page to a PDF document might take some time.

2. Save the new PDF document.

    a. On the File toolbar, click the **Save file** button. 🖫

    b. In the **Save As** dialog box, navigate to the C:\084548Data\Creating PDF Documents folder and click **Save.**

3. Check if the links are working in the PDF file.

    a. In the Everything For Coffee.pdf file, click the **Coffee Makers** link and observe that the Coffee Makers page is displayed.

    b. Click the **Gourmet Beans** link to navigate to that page.

    c. Choose **File→Close** to close the Everything For Coffee.pdf file.

TOPIC D

Create a PDF Document Using Email Applications

You converted web pages to PDF documents. In a typical work environment, you may be exchanging official correspondence with colleagues and clients through email frequently, and you may want to store copies of these in an easily accessible format for future reference. In this topic, you will convert email messages to a PDF document.

Email applications allow you to create archives to store your old messages and to create space in your Inbox or other folders. However, the messages in the archive are not easily searchable. Using the Acrobat options available in email applications, you can save important messages as PDF files, and easily access and retrieve them when required.

PDF Creation Options in Email Applications

Email applications such as Lotus Notes and Microsoft Outlook provide you with options to convert email messages to a PDF document. You can create a PDF file from individual email messages, or convert an email folder to a PDF file. When you choose to convert an email folder, all the messages in the selected folder are converted to PDF. You can either create a PDF file to store your converted messages, or append the message or email folder to the existing PDF files.

Adobe PDF Conversion Buttons in Lotus Notes

If the PDF conversion buttons are not visible on the toolbar in Lotus Notes 8 or later versions, you can customize the toolbar preferences using the **Preferences** dialog box. The conversion buttons allow you to convert specific email messages or folders in Lotus Notes.

How to Create a PDF Document Using Email Applications

Procedure Reference: Convert Lotus Notes Email Messages to a PDF Document

To convert Lotus Notes email messages to a PDF document:

1. Open the Lotus Notes application.
2. Display the folder containing the appropriate message.
3. Select the message you want to convert to a PDF document.
4. On the **Acrobat PDFMaker** toolbar, click the **Convert Selected Message(s) to Adobe PDF** button to convert the selected email message to PDF documents.
5. In the **Save Adobe PDF File As** dialog box, navigate to the location where you want to save the file.
6. If necessary, in the **File name** text box, type a new name for the PDF document.
7. Click **Save.**

Procedure Reference: Convert Microsoft Outlook Email Messages to a PDF Document

To convert Microsoft Outlook email messages to a PDF document:

1. Open the Microsoft Outlook application.

2. Display the folder containing the appropriate message.

3. Select the message you want to convert to a PDF document.

4. On the **Adobe PDF** tab, in the **Convert** group, click the **Selected Messages** button and select **Create New PDF** to convert the selected email message to a PDF document.

5. In the **Save Adobe PDF File As** dialog box, navigate to the location where you want to save the file.

6. If necessary, in the **File name** text box, type a new name for the PDF document.

7. Click **Save.**

Procedure Reference: Convert a Mail Folder to a PDF Document

To convert a mail folder to a PDF document:

1. Open the mail application.

2. On the **Adobe PDF** tab, from the **Selected Folders** drop-down menu, choose **Create New PDF.**

3. In the **Convert folder(s) to PDF** dialog box, check the folders whose contents you want to convert into PDF documents.

4. If necessary, check the **Convert this folder and all sub folders** check box.

5. Click **OK.**

6. In the **Save Adobe PDF File As** dialog box, in the **File name** text box, specify a name for the file.

7. Navigate to the desired location and click **Save** to save the file.

Append to PDF Option in Outlook

You can use the **Append to PDF** option to convert messages and folders in Microsoft Outlook to PDF documents and attach the converted PDF to an existing PDF.

Automatic Archival in Email Applications

Acrobat X Pro provides certain features for automatic archival in Lotus Notes and Microsoft Outlook.

You can archive email messages in Lotus Notes using Acrobat X Pro. The messages or folders you choose for archiving will be converted to PDF and will be saved in the specified location.

In many email applications, if any specific folder size increases, you may not be able to receive or send new messages or store them for future reference. To avoid this, some email applications provide an automatic archival option that allows you to archive old email messages as a file once the folder size reaches a specified size.

Acrobat X Pro provides certain features for automatic archival of email messages in Microsoft Outlook. You can archive email messages by selecting the **Adobe PDF** tab in Microsoft Outlook and by clicking **Setup Automatic Archival.** This will display the **Acrobat PDFMaker** dialog box where you can enable automatic archival and set the frequency of archiving. You can also choose folders that you want to archive periodically. The folders that you archive will be saved as a .pst file.

Acrobat X Pro also provides some features for automatic archival in Lotus Notes. The messages or folders you choose for archiving will be converted to PDF documents and will be saved in the specified location. Once Acrobat X Pro is installed on your system, the **Convert Selected Folder(s) to Adobe PDF** button is added to the Lotus Notes toolbar. You can use this button to archive folders, or you can enable automatic archival by choosing **Actions→Setup Automatic Archival.** You can choose the folders that you want to archive periodically.

Convert Multiple Folders in Microsoft Outlook and Lotus Notes to PDFs

You can convert multiple mail folders in Microsoft Outlook and Lotus Notes to PDFs by checking the required check boxes in the **Convert folder(s) to PDF** dialog box. This dialog box is displayed when you convert mail folders to PDFs.

ACTIVITY 2-4
Creating PDF Documents Using Microsoft Outlook

Data Files:

C:\084548Data\Creating PDF Documents\Outlook.pst, C:\084548Data\Creating PDF Documents\Meeting Agenda.txt

Before You Begin:

 You will need to work in pairs to perform the steps given in the Before You Begin section.

1. Choose **Start→All Programs→Microsoft Office→Microsoft Outlook 2010** to open the Microsoft Office Outlook 2010 application and, in the **Microsoft Office Outlook** message box, click **OK.**

2. Send an email to your partner with the subject "Meeting Agenda" and use the information specified in the C:\084548Data\Creating PDF Documents\Meeting Agenda.txt file as the body of the email. Close the Meeting Agenda.txt file.

 If your email ID is student01@ourglobalcompany.com, then send an email to your partner, student02@ourglobalcompany.com, and let the latter send a reply.

Scenario:

Every day you receive several business email messages. Some you would like to store for future reference, while others you would want to share with your colleagues. But, they should be able to view it irrespective of availability of the mail application.

---

1. Convert the email message from your partner to PDF.

    a. Verify that you received an email message from your partner.

    b. Select the email message you received from your partner.

    c. Select the **Adobe PDF** tab. In the **Convert** group, from the **Selected Messages** drop-down menu, choose **Create New PDF.**

    d. In the **Save Adobe PDF File As** dialog box, navigate to the C:\084548Data\Creating PDF Documents folder.

    e. Verify that in the **File name** text box, the name of the file is displayed as **"Meeting Agenda"** and click **Save.**

    f. Observe that the **Creating Adobe PDF** message box with the progress bar is displayed.

    g. Observe that the email message has been converted to PDF.

    h. Close the Meeting Agenda.pdf file.

i.   Close the Microsoft Outlook application.

2. Which option helps you to create a PDF of a Microsoft Outlook email message?

a) Create New PDF

b) Change Conversion Settings

c) Setup Automatic Archival

d) Selected Messages

TOPIC E

Create a PDF Document Using Acrobat

You created PDF documents from Microsoft Office applications, web pages, and email messages. Now, you may have several documents created in various applications that you want to combine into a PDF document. In this topic, you will create a PDF document using Acrobat.

The ability to combine multiple documents of different formats into a PDF document allows you to organize, store, and share several files as a unit, and in a format that anyone with the free Adobe Reader application can access.

The Combine Files Dialog Box

In Acrobat, you can combine files of different formats and save them as a PDF file within another PDF. The options to combine the files are available in the **Combine Files** dialog box. The **Combine Files** dialog box allows you to add files individually, or add multiple files by selecting the folder containing the files. The dialog box also provides you with options to specify the order in which the files should appear in the newly combined PDF file, the specific pages to be included from a file, and the files to be removed, if any. You can create either a PDF document or a PDF portfolio based on your requirement.

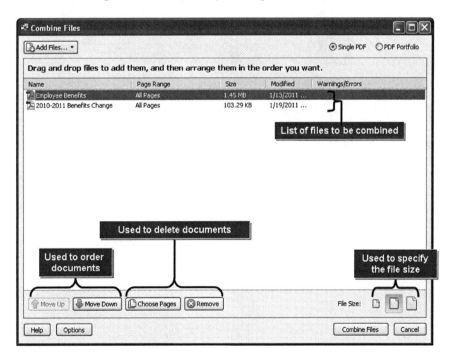

Figure 2-2: Options for combining different file formats.

File Size and Conversion Settings

The **Combine Files** dialog box allows you to choose the file size of the target PDF file or PDF Portfolio. Based on the file size option you select, the conversion settings applied will vary.

File Size Option	Description
Default File Size	Creates a PDF document using the default conversion settings. This setting is suitable for normal viewing and printing of documents.
Larger File Size	Creates a PDF document of high quality using the **High Quality Print** settings.
Smaller File Size	Creates the most optimized output by compressing the file size and by reducing the screen resolution. It makes use of low-quality JPEG images. This setting is suitable for viewing documents on-screen or online. You can also use this setting to optimize files for emailing purposes.

PDF Portfolios

A PDF portfolio is created by combining files of different formats while retaining their original formats in the combined file. The individual files also retain their appearance and page numbering. A PDF portfolio has a cover sheet that provides instructions and information useful to the readers. The original file names can be displayed in the list view by selecting the **Details** panel in the Task pane.

 The default file name assigned to a PDF portfolio is Portfolio1.

The Portfolio Window

Using the options in the PDF portfolio window, you can manipulate the layout and format, and share the contents of a portfolio document. You can add content such as files, new folders, and web content to the portfolio document. You can also define the visual themes, colors, and background of the portfolio using the options in the **Layout** panel.

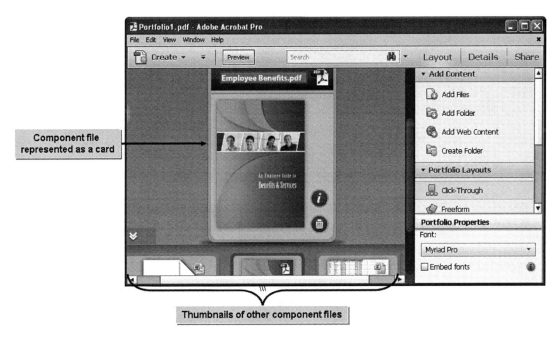

Figure 2-3: Portfolio containing multiple files.

Component	Description
PDF Portfolio toolbar	Provides options for viewing, saving, printing, editing, and searching files within a portfolio.
Component documents and folders area	Displays files and folders contained within the portfolio. The buttons located below the component document and folder area allow you to add files and folders to the portfolio.
Layout panel	Provides options for modifying the portfolio layout, color scheme, visual theme, and file display option. You can also add files to a portfolio, create folders, or add existing folders to a portfolio using the **Layout** panel.
Details panel	Displays details of the files contained in the portfolio.
Share panel	Allows you to email portfolios for reviewing.

The Create PDF Portfolio Dialog Box

You can quickly create PDF portfolios using the various components in the **Create PDF Portfolio** dialog box which is displayed on clicking the **Create** drop-down arrow.

Component	Enables You To
Click-Through	Click the component files to navigate through the PDF portfolio. You can also reorder files using this option.
Freeform	Arrange the component files of a PDF portfolio in a scattered thumbnail placement. You can customize the order and configuration of the files.

Component	Enables You To
Grid	Arrange content in an orderly grid facilitating the accommodation of large numbers of files.
Linear	Arrange files in a linear path and guide the user through each file in a sequence.
Wave	Arrange files in a spinning path that fans out off the screen. This helps you present them in a visually appealing manner.
Import Custom Layout	Import a pre-defined layout that can be included in a portfolio.
Add Files	Add files from folders to create a PDF portfolio.

The Default Layout of Files in a PDF Portfolio

The component file appears as a card in the card pane. The default view also displays the files and folders as thumbnails in the mini-navigator pane below the card pane. Each of the thumbnails can be double-clicked to open and view the individual files in the card pane. You can also add a description of the file or its contents to the thumbnail.

Views Available in a PDF Portfolio

The default views available in a PDF portfolio are as follows: **Cover Sheet, Layout,** and **Details.** The **Cover Sheet** view enables you to set passwords to secure the portfolio document. The **Layout** view displays the card pane, which represents the component files as cards, the mini-navigator pane, the PDF Portfolio toolbar, and the **Layout, Details** and **Share** panels. The **Layout** panel has the PDF portfolio template options that allow you to change the layout of the portfolio document, the **Details** panel lists the files in the portfolio, and the **Share** panel has options that allow you to share files for reviewing. These views can be accessed using the **View** menu or the PDF Portfolio toolbar.

The PDF Portfolio Template Pane

The PDF portfolio template pane consists of customizable layouts, color schemes, and visual themes for a PDF portfolio. The portfolio template helps determine the overall look and feel of a portfolio.

How to Create a PDF Document Using Acrobat

Procedure Reference: Create a PDF Document from a Single File

To create a PDF document from a single file:

1. In Acrobat X Pro, choose **File→Create PDF→PDF From File.**

2. In the **Open** dialog box, from the **Files of type** drop-down list, select the file type you want to convert.

3. Navigate to and select the file you want to convert.

4. If necessary, click the **Settings** button, specify the Adobe PDF conversion settings, and click **OK** to apply the settings.

 The **Settings** button will be inactive if no conversion settings are applied for the selected file type.

5. Click **Open** to convert the file.

Procedure Reference: Create a PDF Document from Multiple Files

To create a PDF document from multiple files:

1. Open the **Combine Files** dialog box.
   - Choose **File→Create→Combine Files into a Single PDF** or;
   - From the **Create** drop-down menu, choose **Combine Files into a Single PDF.**

2. From the **Add Files** drop-down list, select **Add Files.**

3. In the **Add Files** dialog box, select the file you want to add.

4. Click **Add Files** to add the selected files.

5. If necessary, select a document and click **Remove** to remove any of the listed files.

6. If necessary, rearrange the files to reflect the order in which you want them to be displayed in the new PDF.
   - Rearrange the files by manually dragging and dropping them or;
   - Select the file you want to move and click **Move Up** or **Move Down.**

7. If necessary, click **Options** and in the **Options** dialog box, check the desired check boxes to add bookmarks or to convert all files to PDFs when creating the portfolio, and click **OK.**
   - Check the **Always enable accessibility and reflow** check box to facilitate access to the document and reflow of text.
   - Check the **Always add bookmarks to Adobe PDF** check box to add bookmarks to the portfolio document.
   - Check the **Continue combining if an error occurs** check box to enable the application to proceed with merging files even if an error is encountered.
   - Check the **Convert all files to PDF when creating a portfolio** check box to convert files of other formats to PDFs while generating a PDF portfolio.

8. If necessary, in the **Combine Files** dialog box, select the desired file size.
   - Click the **Smaller File Size** button to reduce large images to screen resolution.
   - Click the **Default File Size** button to retain the original file size and quality.
   - Click the **Larger File Size** button to display high resolution text and images.

9. If necessary, select a file, click **Choose Pages** and in the **Preview and Select Page Range** dialog box, in the **Select Page Range** section, select the required pages of the listed files that you want to include in the combined file, and click **OK.**

10. Click **Combine Files** to merge the selected files.

11. If necessary, in the **Save As** dialog box, navigate to the desired location where you want to save the file.

12. In the **File name** text box, type a new file name and click **Save.**

Procedure Reference: Create a PDF Portfolio from Multiple Files

To create a PDF portfolio from multiple files:

1. Open the **Combine Files** dialog box.

2. Select the **PDF Portfolio** option.

3. Choose **Add Files→Add Files.**

4. In the **Add Files** dialog box, navigate to the desired location where you have stored the files and select them.

5. Click **Add Files** to add the selected files.

6. Click **Finish** to create the PDF portfolio.

7. If necessary, choose **File→Save Portfolio** and in the **Save As** dialog box, navigate to the location where you want to save the portfolio file. In the **File name** text box, type a new file name and click **Save** to save the PDF portfolio with a different name.

8. If necessary, convert non-PDF files to PDF documents.

    a. In the component document and folders area, right-click the thumbnail image of the non-pdf file and choose **Convert to PDF.**

    b. In the **Convert to PDF** dialog box, click **OK** to display a PDF version of the file.

Procedure Reference: Convert a Mail Folder into a PDF Portfolio

To convert a mail folder into a PDF portfolio:

1. Display the **Convert folder(s) to PDF** dialog box.

    ● In the Microsoft Outlook application, on the **Acrobat PDFMaker** toolbar, click the **Create Adobe PDF from folders** button.

    ● In the Lotus Notes application, on the **Acrobat PDFMaker** toolbar, click the **Convert Selected Folder(s) to Adobe PDF** button.

2. In the **Convert folder(s) to PDF** dialog box, check the desired folder check boxes.

3. If necessary, check the **Convert this folder and all sub folders** check box.

4. Click **OK** to convert the selected folders to a PDF document.

5. In the **Save Adobe PDF File As** dialog box, navigate to the location where you want to save the file.

6. If necessary, in the **File name** text box, specify a name for the file.

7. Click **Save** to save the file.

8. In the **Creating Adobe PDF** dialog box, click **Close** to display the PDF.

Procedure Reference: Search Across a PDF Portfolio

To search across a PDF portfolio:

1. Open the portfolio in which you want to conduct the search.

2. Choose **Edit→Search Entire Portfolio.**

3. In the **PDF Portfolio** toolbar, in the **Search** text box, type the word you want to search and press **Enter** to display the search results.

4. If necessary, in the **Search Results for This portfolio** pane, click the desired search result to view its occurrence on the document pane.

ACTIVITY 2-5
Combining Multiple Files into a PDF Document

Data Files:

C:\084548Data\Creating PDF Documents\Staff Contacts.xlsx, C:\084548Data\Creating PDF Documents\HR Memo Leave.docx, C:\084548Data\Creating PDF Documents\HR Memo New PPO.docx, C:\084548Data\Creating PDF Documents\HR Memo President's Day.docx

Before You Begin:
The Adobe Acrobat X Pro application is open.

Scenario:
The Employee Benefits.pdf document, which you created to distribute to your staff, reflects recent changes to employee benefits. To ensure that everyone is aware of the policy changes, you want to distribute copies of all memos distributed over the past year describing changes to employee benefits. These memos were initially created in Microsoft Office Word and Excel and were distributed in print form. You would like to combine the memos as a PDF portfolio so that each file appears separately with its own pagination. In order to make it convenient for the employees, you want to generate a document having combined data of both the Employee Benefits document and the memo PDF, so that they can compare the documents and find out the newer benefits available to the employees.

---

1. Generate a merged PDF from the memos.

    a. In the Acrobat X Pro application, choose **File→Create→Combine Files into a Single PDF.**

    b. In the **Combine Files** window, from the **Add Files** drop-down menu, choose **Add Files.**

    c. In the **Add Files** dialog box, navigate to the C:\084548Data\Creating PDF Documents folder.

    d. Select **HR Memo Leave.docx,** hold down **Shift,** and select the **HR Memo President's Day.docx** file.

    e. Hold down **Ctrl,** select the **Staff Contacts.xlsx** file and click **Add Files.**

    f. In the **Combine Files** window, click below the Staff Contacts file to deselect all files.

    g. Select **HR Memo President's Day.**

    h. Click **Move Up** twice to move the **HR Memo President's Day** file above the **HR Memo Leave** file.

    i. Click **Combine Files.**

 The process of combining the files into a single PDF might take some time.

j. Observe that the combined PDF document is generated with the default name Binder1.pdf.

k. Choose **File→Save.**

l. In the **Save As** dialog box, in the **File name** text box, type *2010–2011 Benefits Changes* and click **Save.**

m. Scroll down to view the combined document.

2. Combine the PDF with the Employee Benefits document.

a. Choose **File→Create→Combine Files into a Single PDF.**

b. In the **Combine Files** window, select the **PDF Portfolio** option.

c. From the **Add Files** drop-down menu, choose **Add Files.**

d. Select **HR Memo Leave.docx, HR Memo New PPO.docx, HR Memo President's Day.docx,** and **Staff Contacts.xlsx.**

e. In the **Add Files** dialog box, click **Add Files.**

f. Observe that the selected files are displayed in the **Combine Files** window.

g. Click **Create PDF Portfolio.**

h. Observe that the combined PDF document is generated with a default name.

i. In the Adobe Acrobat Pro window, double-click **HR Memo Leave.pdf**

j. Observe that the content of the HR Memo Leave.pdf document is displayed.

k. Close the HR Memo Leave.pdf document.

3. Save the PDF portfolio.

a. In the Adobe Acrobat Pro window, choose **File→Save Portfolio.**

b. In the **Save As** dialog box, in the **File name** text box, type *2010–2011 Benefits Changes Portfolio* and then click **Save.**

c. Close all open PDF files.

Lesson 2 Follow-up

In this lesson, you converted files from other applications to PDF. This enables you to share your documents and information with a global audience.

1. **Which techniques will you use for generating PDF documents? Why?**

2. **What are the benefits of converting documents of other file formats to a PDF?**

3 Navigating to a Specific Content in a PDF Document

Lesson Time: 60 minutes

Lesson Objectives:

In this lesson, you will navigate to and search for a specific content in a PDF document.

You will:

● Perform a search in a PDF document.

● Use bookmarks to navigate to a specific location within a PDF document.

● Create links within a PDF document.

Introduction

You created a PDF document. Now, you may need to navigate to a specific content in the document. In this lesson, you will include navigational elements in a PDF document.

Locating a specific topic in a multi-page document may require users to scroll through the entire document. This could be tedious and time consuming. If navigation aids are included in it, users can directly navigate to the information they want to locate.

TOPIC A
Perform a Search

You created PDF documents. At times, you may feel it is necessary to locate certain words or phrases that are not immediately apparent. In this topic, you will search a PDF document.

Sometimes, you may need to find all instances of a particular word or phrase in a PDF document. It is easy to search for instances of a word or phrase in a document containing few pages, whereas documents that run about hundred pages may take hours to get done, and you may miss some instances. Instead, you can use the search options of Acrobat X Pro for quick and accurate results.

The Search Window

Searching a PDF document will allow you to quickly locate what you are looking for in the document. You can use the Search window to search for a word or phrase in the current document and across multiple PDF documents. You can search for whole words, case-sensitive words, bookmarks, comments, layers, form fields, digital signatures, metadata, and attachments. The search results can be saved in either the PDF or CSV file format. You can edit CSV files using common spreadsheet applications such as Microsoft Excel.

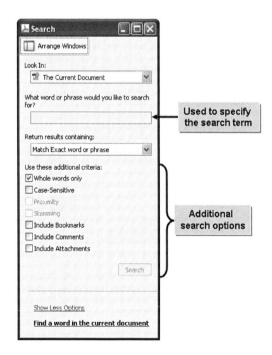

Figure 3-1: The Advanced Search options.

The CSV Format
Comma Separated Values (CSV) is a special type of text file format which stores large volumes of database information or spreadsheet information in a simple way with each record on a separate line and each field within the record separated by comma.

Search Preferences

Search options allow you to either broaden or restrict your search. You can set the search options in the **Preferences** dialog box by selecting the **Search** option in the **Categories** section.

How to Perform a Search

Procedure Reference: Perform a Search Using the Find Toolbar

To perform a search using the **Find** toolbar:

1. If necessary, choose **Edit→Find** to display the **Find** toolbar.
2. In the **Find** text box, type the text you want to search for.
3. If necessary, click the **Find** drop-down arrow and choose any of the commands to refine the search.
4. Press **Enter** to begin the search.
5. Find the other instances of the text you searched for.
    *   Continue to press **Enter** to locate the next instances of the search text or;
    *   On the **Find** toolbar, click the **Find Previous** or **Find Next** button to locate the previous or next instances of the text.
6. In the **Adobe Acrobat** message box, click **OK** to close it.

Procedure Reference: Perform a Search Using the Search Window

To perform a search using the Search window:

1. Choose **Edit→Advanced Search** to display the Search window.
2. If necessary, in the **Where would you like to search** section, specify whether you want to search for a word or phrase in the current PDF document or in all PDF documents in a specific location on your computer.
3. In the **What word or phrase would you like to search for** text box, type the word or phrase you want to locate.
4. If necessary, specify additional search parameters using the check boxes in the Search window.
5. In the Search window, click **Search.**
6. In the **Results** list box, expand the documents listed to view all occurrences of the word in the document.
7. Navigate to each occurrence of the word.
    *   In the **Results** list box, click any occurrence of the word to display that instance of the word with a highlight.
    *   Press **Ctrl+G** to move to the next occurrence, or press **Ctrl+Shift+G** to move to the previous occurrence.
    *   Choose **Edit→Search Results** and then choose any of the commands to navigate to the next or previous occurrence of the word, or to navigate to the next or previous document containing occurrences of the word you searched for.
8. If necessary, specify the additional search options by selecting **More Options** in the Search window.
9. If necessary, from the **Save results to file** drop-down menu, choose the desired command to save the search results in the PDF or CSV file format.

10. If necessary, in the Search window, click **New Search** and search for another word.

11. Once the search is complete, close the Search window.

ACTIVITY 3-1
Searching for Specific Words and Topics in Acrobat

Data Files:

C:\084548Data\Navigating to Specific Content\Employee Benefits.pdf

Scenario:

You read through a few articles in the Employee Benefits guide, but you do not have time to continue with the rest. However, you are curious to read about the new benefits announced in the guide and to know if the Employee Benefits guide mentions anything about this year's insurance plan for the employees.

---

1. Locate all instances of the word "benefits" in the document using the **Find** toolbar.

   a. From the C:\084548Data\Navigating to Specific Content folder, open the Employee Benefits.pdf file.

   b. Choose **Edit→Find.**

   c. On the **Find** toolbar, in the text box, type *benefits*

   d. Click the **Find** drop-down arrow, select **Whole Words Only,** and press **Enter** to begin the search.

   e. Observe that the first instance of the word "benefits" is highlighted in the document pane.

   f. On the **Find** toolbar, click the **Find next** button eight times to complete the search.

   g. On the **Find** toolbar, continue to click the **Find Next** button to locate any other instance of the word "benefits."

   h. In the **Adobe Acrobat** message box, click **OK.**

   i. Close the **Find** toolbar.

---

2. Find all instances of the word "plans" using the Search window.

   a. Choose **Edit→Advanced Search** to display the Search window.

   b. In the **What word or phrase would you like to search for** text box, type *plans*

   c. Click **Search** to locate instances of the word "plans."

   d. Observe that in the Search window, in the **Results** section, there are more than one instance of the word "plans" highlighted and, in the document pane, the word "Plans" is highlighted.

   e. In the **Results** section, click any of the highlighted word "plans" to navigate to the highlighted word in the document pane.

---

3. Save the search results as a CSV file.

---

a.   In the Search window, from the **Save results to file** drop-down menu, ⊟˙ choose **Save results to CSV.**

b.   In the **Save Search Results** dialog box, in the **File name** text box, type *Plans* and click **Save.**

c.   In Windows Explorer, navigate to the C:\084548Data\Navigating to Specific Content folder and open the Plans.csv file.

d.   Observe that the search results are exported and saved in the CSV file format.

e.   Close the Microsoft Excel application.

f.   Close Windows Explorer.

g.   Close the Search window.

TOPIC B
Manage Bookmarks

You searched for words in a PDF document. Now, you may need to facilitate users to jump to specific locations in a document. In this topic, you will use bookmarks.

When you have a PDF document with many pages, it is helpful to include information similar to that of a table of contents. Bookmarks not only provide a list of topics similar to those in a table of contents, but also allow users to navigate directly to the topic of interest. They help you make this information accessible across all pages of a document, rather than at the beginning of a document.

Bookmarks

Definition:

A *bookmark* is a text entry that you can click to navigate to a predetermined location within a PDF document. Bookmarks can link to pages, or content within the current PDF document or other PDF documents. They can also be linked to a website. In addition, bookmarks can perform actions such as executing a menu command, opening a file, and reading an article.

Example:

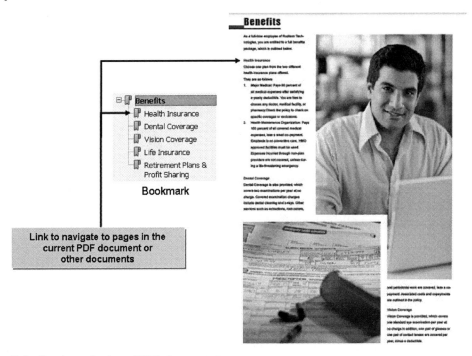

Figure 3-2: Bookmarks in a PDF document.

The Bookmarks Panel

The **Bookmarks** panel is used to list the bookmarks available in a PDF document. There are a number of components in the **Bookmarks** panel: **Delete Bookmark, New bookmark, Expand current bookmark, Options,** and much more. The **Options** drop-down menu can be used to expand or collapse the content of bookmarks, hide bookmarks, highlight bookmarks, change the text size of bookmarks, change bookmark destinations, rename bookmarks, and wrap long bookmarks. You can also change the appearance of bookmarks using the **Properties** command.

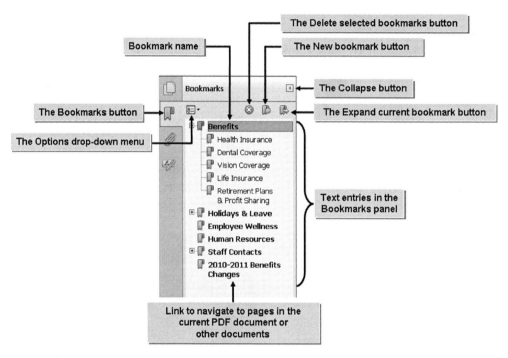

Figure 3-3: Components of the Bookmarks panel.

The Selection Tool

Using the Selection tool on the **Select & Zoom** toolbar, you can select various types of PDF content. The content that can be selected includes text, images, and tables in a PDF document.

How to Use Bookmarks

Procedure Reference: Create a Bookmark

To create a bookmark:

1. In the document pane, scroll to view the page section of the document you want the bookmark to link to.

2. Create a bookmark.

   - Create a bookmark using the **Bookmarks** panel.

     a. On the **Select & Zoom** toolbar, select the Selection tool, and click and drag to select the text in the document you want the bookmark to link to.

     b. If necessary, in the **Navigation Pane,** click the **Bookmarks** button to display the **Bookmarks** panel.

     c. At the top of the **Bookmarks** panel, click the **New bookmark** or from the **Options** drop-down menu, choose **New Bookmark.**

     d. Type the desired name for the bookmark and press **Enter.**

   - Create a bookmark using the Selection tool.

     a. On the **Select & Zoom** toolbar, select the Selection tool, and click and drag to select the text in the document you want the bookmark to link to.

     b. Right-click the selection and choose **Add Bookmark.**

     c. The bookmark will be added to the **Bookmarks** panel, and its name will match the text you selected in the document. If necessary, rename the bookmark and press **Enter.**

3. If necessary, nest bookmarks.

   a. In the **Bookmarks** panel, select one or more bookmark icons to be nested.

   b. Nest the bookmarks.

      - Click and drag the selected bookmark icons, and when the line is displayed directly below the intended parent bookmark name, release the mouse button.

 If the line is displayed directly below the parent bookmark icon, the bookmark will not be nested. It has to be displayed beneath the parent bookmark name to be nested.

      - Cut the bookmarks to be nested, select the desired parent bookmark, and from the **Options** drop-down menu, choose **Paste under Selected Bookmark.**

   c. If necessary, remove the nesting for the bookmarks.

      - Click and drag the nested bookmarks above or below the bookmark icon of any non-nested bookmark or;

      - Cut the nested bookmark, select a bookmark, from the **Options** drop-down menu, and choose **Paste after Selected Bookmark.**

4. If necessary, in the **Bookmarks** panel, click the desired bookmark to navigate to a specific location.

5. If necessary, select a bookmark and press **Delete,** or in the **Bookmarks** panel, click the **Delete selected bookmarks** button to delete the bookmark.

Procedure Reference: Change a Bookmark's Destination

To change a bookmark's destination:

1. In the **Bookmarks** panel, select the bookmark the destination of which you want to change.

2. Navigate to the desired destination.

3. Change the bookmark's destination.
   - In the **Bookmarks** panel, right-click the bookmark and choose **Set Destination** or;
   - In the **Bookmarks** panel, from the **Options** drop-down menu, choose **Set Bookmark Destination.**

4. In the **Adobe Acrobat** dialog box, click **Yes** to change the bookmark's destination.

Procedure Reference: Add an Action to a Bookmark

To add an action to a bookmark:

1. Open the **Bookmark Properties** dialog box for the bookmark the action of which you want to modify.
   - Right-click the bookmark and choose **Properties** or;
   - Select the bookmark and from the **Options** drop-down menu, choose **Properties.**

2. Select the **Actions** tab.

3. In the **Add an Action** section, from the **Select Action** drop-down list, select an action type and click **Add.**

4. Specify the desired options for the selected action.

5. In the **Bookmark Properties** dialog box, click **OK.**

6. If necessary, modify a bookmark's action.
   a. Display the **Bookmark Properties** dialog box.
   b. Select the **Action** tab and in the **Actions** section, in the list box, select an action and click **Edit.**
   c. In the **Go to a page in this document** dialog box, specify the settings in the **Options** section.
      - Select **Use Page Number,** type the page number to which you want to reassign the action and then from the **Zoom** drop-down list, select an option.
      - Select **Use Named Destination,** click **Browse** and, in the **Choose Destination** dialog box, select a destination and click **OK.**
   d. In the **Go to a page in this document** dialog box, click **OK** to apply the settings.
   e. In the **Bookmark Properties** dialog box, click **OK** to apply the settings.

Procedure Reference: Change a Bookmark's Formatting

To change a bookmark's formatting:

1. In the **Bookmarks** panel, select one or more bookmarks to be formatted.

2. Open the **Bookmark Properties** dialog box.

3. Select the **Appearance** tab.

4. Change the bookmark's formatting.
   - From the **Style** drop-down list, select a formatting style.
   - Click the **Color** box and select a color.

5. Click **OK.**

6. If necessary, from the **Options** drop-down menu, choose **Collapse Top-Level Book-marks.**

7. If necessary, set the changed format as the default setting for new bookmarks.

    ●   Select the bookmark for which you changed the formatting and from the **Options** drop-down menu, choose **Use Current Appearance as New Default** or;

    ●   Right-click the bookmark for which you changed the formatting and choose **Use Current Appearance as New Default.**

8. If necessary, display the full name of a long bookmark.

    ●   Right-click the bookmark and choose **Wrap Long Bookmarks** or;

    ●   From the **Options** drop-down menu, choose **Wrap Long Bookmarks.**

ACTIVITY 3-2
Adding Bookmarks to the Benefits Guide

Before You Begin:
The Employee Benefits.pdf file is open.

Scenario:
The main headings on each page are bookmarked in the Employee Benefits.pdf document. You also want to bookmark the subheadings so that users can quickly locate the information they want. You want each heading bookmark to be formatted such that it is distinct from the sub-heading bookmarks within it. You also want to add an additional bookmark that navigates to another document, which contains the recent updates to the Employee Benefits.pdf file.

---

1. Add bookmarks to the subheadings on pages 4 and 5.

   a. In the **Navigation Pane,** click the Bookmarks button.

   b. In the **Bookmarks** panel, verify that the **Benefits** bookmark is selected.

   c. In the document pane, triple-click the subheading "Health Insurance" to select it.

   d. Right-click the "Health Insurance" subheading, choose **Add Bookmark,** and press **Enter.**

   e. In the document pane, triple-click the subheading "Dental Coverage" to select it.

   f. Right-click the "Dental Coverage" subheading, choose **Add Bookmark,** and press **Enter.**

   g. In the document pane, scroll down and triple-click the subheading "Vision Coverage" to select it.

   h. Right-click the "Vision Coverage" subheading, choose **Add Bookmark,** and press **Enter.**

   i. On the Page Navigation toolbar, click the **Show next page** button.

   j. In the document pane, triple-click the subheading "Life Insurance" to select it.

   k. Right-click the "Life Insurance" subheading, choose **Add Bookmark,** and press **Enter.**

   l. In the document pane, scroll down, triple-click the subheading "Retirement Plans & Profit Sharing" to select it.

   m. Right-click the "Retirement Plans & Profit Sharing" subheading, choose **Add Book-mark,** and press **Enter.**

---

2. Add bookmarks for the subheadings on the rest of the pages.

   a. In the **Bookmarks** panel, click the **Holidays & Leave** bookmark.

   b. Create bookmarks for the subheadings in the "Holidays & Leave" section of the page.

---

3. Organize the subheading bookmarks so that they are nested within their respective parent bookmarks.

    a. In the **Bookmarks** panel, click the **Health Insurance** bookmark.

    b. Hold down **Shift** and click **Retirement Plans & Profit Sharing** to select the bookmarks.

    c. Right-click the selected bookmarks and choose **Cut.**

    d. Click the **Benefits** bookmark, right-click, and choose **Paste under Selected Bookmark.**

    e. Observe the changes in the **Bookmarks** panel.

    f. In the **Bookmarks** panel, click the **Paid Holidays** bookmark.

    g. Hold down **Shift** and click the **Extended Maternity/Paternity Leave** bookmark to select the bookmarks.

    h. Nest the selected bookmarks under the **Holidays & Leave** bookmark.

4. Apply bold formatting to the heading bookmarks.

    a. In the **Bookmarks** panel, from the **Options** drop-down menu, choose **Collapse Top-Level Bookmarks.**

    b. In the **Bookmarks** panel, click the **Benefits** bookmark.

    c. Hold down **Shift** and click the **Staff Contacts** to select the heading bookmarks.

    d. In the **Bookmarks** panel, from the **Options** drop-down menu, choose **Properties.**

    e. In the **Bookmark Properties** dialog box, on the **Appearance** tab, from the **Style** drop-down list, select **Bold.**

    f. Click **OK** to apply bold formatting.

    g. In the **Bookmarks** panel, from the **Options** drop-down menu, choose **Expand Top-Level Bookmarks.**

    h. Observe that only the parent bookmarks are in bold and that the subheading bookmarks are nested within their respective parent bookmarks.

5. Add a new bookmark that has the same formatting as the heading bookmarks.

    a. Click the **Employee Wellness** bookmark.

    b. Right-click the **Employee Wellness** bookmark and choose **Use Current Appearance as New Default** to apply the current formatting to any new bookmarks to be added.

    c. At the top of the **Bookmarks** panel, click the **New bookmark** button.

    d. Type *2010-2011 Benefits Change* and press **Enter** to rename the bookmark.

6. Link the new bookmark to the 2010–2011 Benefits Change.pdf file.

    a. Right-click the **2010-2011 Benefits Change** bookmark and choose **Properties.**

    b. In the **Bookmark Properties** dialog box, select the **Actions** tab.

      c.   In the **Add an Action** section, from the **Select Action** drop-down list, select **Go to a page view** and click **Add.**

      d.   Choose **File→Open.**

      e.   Select the **2010–2011 Benefits Change.pdf** file and click **Open.**

      f.   In the **Create Go to View** dialog box, click **Set Link** to create a link to the 2010–2011 Benefits Change.pdf document.

      g.   In the **Bookmark Properties** dialog box, click **OK.**

      h.   Switch to the 2010–2011 Benefits Change.pdf file.

      i.   Close the 2010–2011 Benefits Change.pdf file.

      j.   In the **Bookmarks** panel, select the **Employee Wellness** bookmark.

      k.   Save the Employee Benefits.pdf file.

---

7.   Test the action bookmark you created.

      a.   In the **Bookmarks** panel, click the **2010–2011 Benefits Change** bookmark.

      b.   Observe that the 2010–2011 Benefits Change.pdf file is displayed.

      c.   Close the 2010–2011 Benefits Change.pdf file.

TOPIC C
Work with Links

You are familiar with using bookmarks. There are other types of navigation aids that are included in the pages of a PDF document. In this topic, you will create links.

When you browse through the contents of a PDF document, you may come across some information that cannot be explained in that location, but may have a comprehensive explanation elsewhere in the same PDF document. It will be helpful to navigate to that location where the explanation is available and read it at once rather than later. Using links, you can create navigation aids for such information.

Links

A *link* is an item within a PDF document which you can click to navigate to another location within the current PDF document, to specific content in another PDF document, or to a web resource. Links are typically displayed as text or graphics within a PDF document. Text links are formatted to appear distinct from the surrounding text.

Edit a link

You can edit links by specifying the various settings to change the hotspot area or the associated link action, delete or resize the link rectangle, or change the destination of the link.

Destinations

Definition:

A *destination* is the end point of a link and is represented by text. Destinations enable navigation paths to be set across a collection of PDF documents. Unlike a link to a page, a link to a destination is not affected by addition or deletion of pages within the target document.

Example:

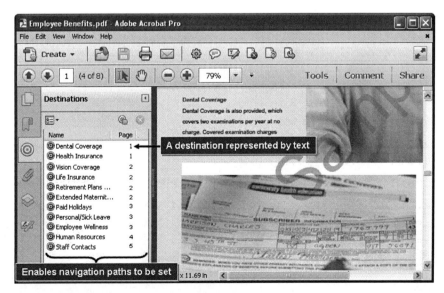

Figure 3-4: Destinations marked in a PDF document.

The Link Properties Dialog Box

The **Link Properties** dialog box has two tabs displaying a number of options for specifying the settings for links. The **Appearance** tab allows you to specify the desired color, link type, line style, line thickness, and style option for each link. The **Actions** tab allows you to execute a menu, navigate to a multimedia view or a particular page, open a file or web page, play sound and media, reset a form, run a JavaScript, set the layer visibility, show or hide a field, and submit a form. You can check the **Locked** check box in the dialog box to lock the settings so that others are not allowed to modify the settings specified for the links.

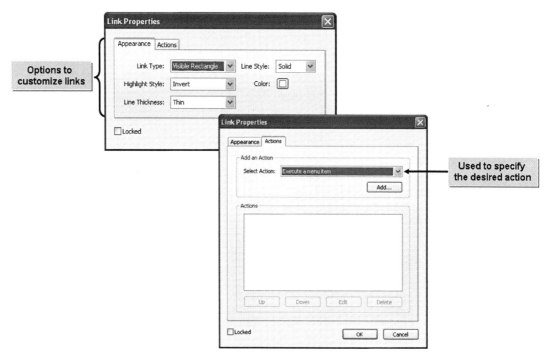

Figure 3-5: Components of the Link Properties dialog box.

How to Work with Links

Procedure Reference: Create a Link

To create a link:

1. Navigate to the text you want to use as a link.

2. Open the **Create Link** dialog box.

    *   Select the text using the Selection tool, right-click the selection, and choose **Create Link** or;

    *   Choose **Tools→Content→Link** and draw a rectangle around the text or;

    *   Choose **Edit→Take a Snapshot** command and, in the **Adobe Acrobat** message box, click **OK,** right-click the selection, and choose **Create Link.**

3. If necessary, in the **Link Appearance** section, specify the appearance of the link.

    *   From the **Link Type** drop-down list, select the desired option to display or hide the rectangle around the link.

    *   From the **Line Style** drop-down list, select an option to specify a particular line style for the link.

    *   From the **Highlight Style** drop-down list, select the required style to highlight the link when it is selected.

    *   Click the link **color box** to display the link color palette and select the desired color to specify a color for the link.

    *   From the **Line Thickness** drop-down list, select the required thickness for the link.

 The **Line Style, Color,** and **Line Thickness** options are not available if **Invisible Rectangle** is selected as the **Link Type.**

4. In the **Link Action** section, specify the action for the link.

    *   Select the **Go to a page view** option to open the link at a specific location on a page, click **Next,** scroll to the required location, and, in the **Create Go To View** message box, click **Set Link.**

    *   Select the **Open a file** option to open the link as a file, click **Next,** navigate to and select the destination file and then click **Select.** If necessary, in the **Specify Open Preference** dialog box, select the desired option to indicate how the document should be opened and click **OK.**

    *   Select the **Open a Web Page** option to open the link as a web page, click **Next,** and in the **Edit URL** text box, type the URL of the destination web page and then click **OK.**

    *   Select the **Custom Link** option to create a custom link, click **Next,** and in the **Link Properties** dialog box, select the **Actions** tab and then set the actions associated with the link.

 The **Custom Link** option is not available for links created using the Selection tool or the **Snapshot** tool.

5. On the **Select & Zoom** toolbar, select the Hand tool.

6. Click the link to navigate to the linked information.

Procedure Reference: Create a Destination

To create a destination:

1. In the target document, navigate to the location where you want to create a destination.

2. Choose **View→Show/Hide→Navigation Panes→Destinations.**

3. Create a destination.

    *   In the **Destinations** panel, from the **Options** drop-down menu, choose **New Destination** or;

    *   At the top of the **Destination** panel, click the **Create new destination** button.

4. Type a name for the destination and press **Enter.**

5. Save the file and close the **Destinations** panel.

Procedure Reference: Duplicate a Link

To duplicate a link:

1. Create a duplicate of a link.

    - Create a duplicate of the original link on the same page.

        a. Select the link using the **Link** tool.

        b. Hold down **Ctrl** and drag the link to the location where you want the new link. As you drag the link, hold down **Shift** to constrain the movement horizontally or vertically.

    - Create a duplicate of a link on a different page from the original link.

        a. Select the link using the **Link** tool.

        b. Choose **Edit→Copy** and navigate to the page where you want the new link.

        c. Choose **Edit→Paste** and drag the rectangle to the text you want to act as a link.

2. If necessary, open the **Link Properties** dialog box, delete the existing action, specify a different one, and click **OK** for the duplicate link to navigate to a different destination.

Procedure Reference: Remove the Visible Border from Links

To remove the visible borders from links:

1. Select the links.

2. Choose **View→Show/Hide→Toolbar Items→Properties Bar.**

3. On the **Properties** toolbar, click **Line Style** and choose **No Line.**

4. Close the **Properties** toolbar.

ACTIVITY 3-3
Creating Links in the Benefits Guide

Scenario:

Although you created bookmarks to navigate to different sections of the Employee Benefits guide, some employees may not be aware of the **Bookmarks** panel. Also, some people may not want to display the **Bookmarks** panel because it leaves less screen space for the document itself. For those who do not use the **Bookmarks** panel, you want to provide an alternate way to quickly navigate to specific content in the document.

1. Create a link for the text "Benefits" on the **Contents** page.

    a. From the C:\084548Data\Navigating to Specific Content folder, open the Employee Benefits.pdf file.

    b. Set the zoom percentage of the document to 75.

    c. On the **Page Navigation** toolbar, click in the Current Page text box, type *2* and then press **Enter.**

    d. In the **Tools** panel, in the **Content** section, in the **Add or Edit Interactive Object** section, click **Link.**

    e. Draw a rectangle around the text "Benefits."

    f. In the **Create Link** dialog box, in the **Link Appearance** section, verify that in the **Link Type** drop-down list, **Visible Rectangle** is selected and in the **Highlight Style** drop-down list, verify that **Invert** is selected.

    g. In the **Link Appearance** section, click the color box to open the color palette and select the white color.

    h. From the **Link Type** drop-down list, select **Invisible Rectangle.**

    i. From the **Highlight Style** drop-down list, select **None.**

    j. In the **Link Action** section, select the **Custom link** option and click **Next.**

    k. In the **Link Properties** dialog box, select the **Actions** tab.

    l. In the **Add an Action** section, from the **Select Action** drop-down list, select **Go to a page view** and click **Add.**

    m. Navigate to page 3.

    n. In the **Create Go to View** dialog box, click **Set Link.**

    o. In the **Link Properties** dialog box, click **OK.**

2. Check the link you created.

    a. Select the Selection tool.

    b. Click the **Benefits** link.

      c.   Observe that the link helps you navigate to the page that contains information on employee benefits.

      d.   Save the file.

3.   Create destinations for all subheadings in the document.

      a.   Scroll down until the "Health Insurance" heading is displayed at the top of the document window.

      b.   Choose **View→Show/Hide→Navigation Panes→Destinations.**

      c.   At the top of the **Destinations** panel, click the **Create new destination** button, type *Health Insurance* and then press **Enter.**

      d.   Scroll down the page until the "Dental Coverage" heading is displayed at the top of the document window.

      e.   In the **Destinations** panel, click the **Create new destination** button, type *Dental Coverage* and then press **Enter.**

      f.   Click the **Collapse** button to collapse the **Destinations** panel.

4.   Create a link for the text "Health Insurance" on the **Contents** page.

      a.   On the **Page Navigation** toolbar, click in the **Current Page** text box, type *2* and then press **Enter.**

      b.   In the **Tools** panel, in the **Content** section, in the **Add or Edit Interactive Object** section, click **Link.**

      c.   Draw a rectangle around the "Health Insurance" subheading.

      d.   In the **Create Link** dialog box, in the **Link Action** section, verify that the **Custom link** option is selected.

      e.   Click **Next.**

      f.   In the **Link Properties** dialog box, select the **Actions** tab.

      g.   From the **Select Action** drop-down list, select **Go to a page view** and click **Add.**

      h.   In the **Create Go To View** dialog box, click **Set Link.**

      i.   In the **Link Properties** dialog box, select the **Actions** tab.

      j.   In the **Actions** section, click **Edit.**

      k.   In the **Go to a page in this document** dialog box, in the **Options** section, select the **Use Named Destination** option and then click **Browse.**

      l.   In the **Choose Destination** dialog box, in the **Select a destination** list box, select **Health Insurance** and click **OK.**

      m.   In the **Go to a page in this document** dialog box, click **OK** to close it.

      n.   In the **Link Properties** dialog box, click **OK** to close it.

      o.   On the **Select & Zoom** toolbar, select the Selection tool and click the **Health Insurance** link.

p. Observe that the link navigates to the page that contains information on "Health Insurance."

5. Duplicate the link you created for the "Health Insurance" subheading.

a. In the **Tools** panel, in the **Content** section, in the **Add or Edit Interactive Object** section, click **Link.**

b. In the document pane, scroll up and select the **Health Insurance** link.

c. Press **Ctrl+Shift** and then drag the **Health Insurance** link onto the **Dental Coverage** link.

d. Double-click the duplicated link.

e. In the **Link Properties** dialog box, select the **Actions** tab.

f. In the **Actions** section, click **Edit.**

g. In the **Go to a page in this document** dialog box, in the **Options** section, verify that the **Use Named Destination** option is selected and click **Browse.**

h. In the **Choose Destination** dialog box, verify that **Dental Coverage** is selected and click **OK.**

i. In the **Go to a page in this document** dialog box, click **OK.**

j. In the **Link Properties** dialog box, click **OK** to close it.

k. Save the file.

l. On the **Select & Zoom** toolbar, select the Selection tool and click the **Dental Coverage** link.

m. Observe that the link navigates to the page that contains information on Dental Coverage.

n. Close the Employee Benefits.pdf file.

Lesson 3 Follow-up

In this lesson, you conducted a simple search within a PDF document, and created and modified bookmarks and links as well. This will enable you to directly navigate to the information you want to view.

1. **Which Search method will you choose to effectively search for a particular word in a PDF document?**

2. **Which method will you prefer to navigate to in a PDF document? Why?**

4 Updating PDF Documents

Lesson Time: 60 minutes

Lesson Objectives:

In this lesson, you will update PDF documents.

You will:

- Manipulate the pages in a PDF document.
- Edit content in a PDF document.
- Add page elements to specific page ranges within a PDF document.
- Extract content from a PDF document.

Introduction

You navigated to a specific content in a PDF document. After generating a PDF document from an authoring application, you may need to edit the content in it such as replacing certain words without using the authoring application. In this lesson, you will use Acrobat X Pro to modify a PDF document to include the contents you want.

Generating a new PDF file from the source file could be difficult and time consuming whenever you want to make changes to a document. Acrobat minimizes the effort required to revise and update your PDF documents by allowing you to directly make changes in the existing PDF document.

TOPIC A
Manipulate PDF Document Pages

You navigated to a specific content in a PDF document. Now, you may need to add, rearrange, or remove pages in a PDF document. In this topic, you will customize pages in a PDF document according to your requirement.

Acrobat allows you to include and exclude pages or contents from a PDF document. By extracting or replacing images or text, you can update a PDF document according to specific requirements.

The Pages Section

The **Pages** section that is available in the **Tools** panel consists of various buttons that can be used to customize and manipulate pages of a PDF document.

Button	Used To
Rotate	Change the view of a page in 90 degree increments.
Delete	Delete one or more pages from a PDF document. However, all pages cannot be deleted. At least, one page must be retained.
Extract	Extract selected pages from a PDF document and generate a new PDF file with only the selected pages. When you extract a page from a PDF document, all links associated with the page are also extracted. However, bookmarks and articles associated with the pages are not extracted. Before extracting pages, a copy of the original document could be saved for future reference.
Replace	Replace an entire PDF page with another PDF page. When a page is replaced, only the text and images on the original page are replaced. Similarly, bookmarks and links that are associated with the replacement page are not carried over.
Crop	Adjust the crop margins of a PDF document using the options in the **Set Page Boxes** dialog box.
Split Document	Split a PDF document into multiple smaller documents. You can specify the maximum number of pages, maximum size of the file, and the bookmarks that you want to include in the documents after splitting it.
Insert from File	Insert pages from one PDF document into another.
More Insert Options	Add pages from a clipboard, web page, or scanner.

The Page Thumbnails Panel

The **Page Thumbnails** panel displays thumbnails of individual pages of a PDF document. You can use the **Options** drop-down menu in the panel to insert, replace, extract, crop, rotate, or delete a page in a PDF document. However, when you change the page numbering using the thumbnails, the page numbers in the document are not modified.

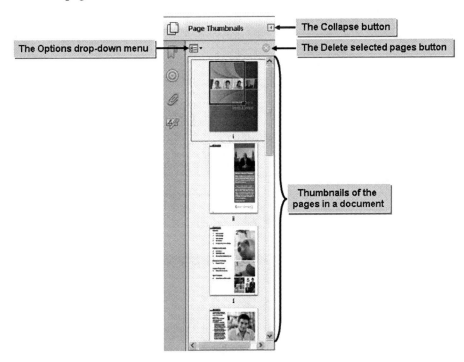

Figure 4-1: Components of the Page Thumbnails panel.

Page Numbering

Page numbering is used to identify the page you are currently viewing when you navigate through a PDF document. The **Page Thumbnails** panel can be used to renumber a specific number of pages without changing the actual page numbering of the document. You can navigate to a specific page by entering the page number in the Current Page text box on the **Page Navigation** toolbar.

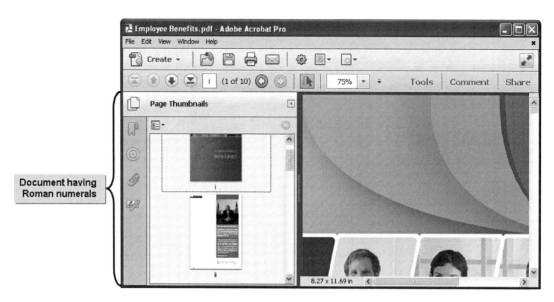

Figure 4-2: Page numbering in a PDF document.

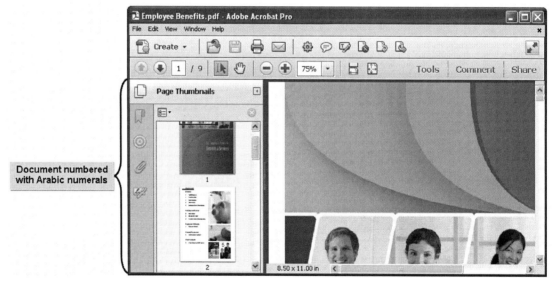

Figure 4-3: Different page numbering styles to choose from.

How to Manipulate PDF Document Pages

Procedure Reference: Insert Pages from One PDF Document to Another

To insert pages from one PDF document to another:

1. Open the PDF document in which you want to add the pages.

2. Specify the source from which you want to insert pages.

    ● Display the **Insert Pages** dialog box to insert pages from a file.

        ■ In the **Tools** panel, in the **Pages** section, in the **Insert Pages** section, click **Insert from File** to display the **Select File To Insert** dialog box. Select the desired file and click **Select** or;

        ■ Display the **Page Thumbnails** panel. From the **Options** drop-down menu, choose **Insert Pages→From File** to display the **Select File To Insert** dialog box. Select the desired file and click **Select.**

    ● Display the **Insert Pages** dialog box to insert pages from copied selection.

        ■ In the **Tools** panel, in the **Pages** section, in the **Insert Pages** section, from the **More Insert Options** drop-down menu, choose **Insert from Clipboard** or;

        ■ In the **Navigation Pane,** click the **Page Thumbnails** button and from the **Options** drop-down menu, choose **Insert Pages→From Clipboard.**

3. In the **Insert Pages** dialog box, specify the order in which you want the inserted pages to be displayed.

    a. From the **Location** drop-down list, select an option to insert the pages before or after the desired page.

    b. In the **Page** section, select the **First, Last,** or **Page** option to insert the desired page.

4. In the **Insert Pages** dialog box, click **OK.**

5. If necessary, scroll down the PDF document to check if the inserted pages appear in the required order.

6. If necessary, save the document with a different name.

Procedure Reference: Delete Pages from a PDF Document

To delete pages from a PDF document:

1. Open the PDF document from which you want to delete the pages.

2. Navigate to the page you want to delete.

3. Display the **Delete Pages** dialog box.

    ● In the **Navigation Pane,** click the **Page Thumbnails** button and from the **Options** drop-down menu, choose **Delete Pages** or;

    ● In the **Page Thumbnails** panel, right-click the thumbnail of the page you want to delete and choose **Delete Pages** or;

    ● In the **Tools** panel, in the **Pages** section, click **Delete.**

4. In the **Delete Pages** dialog box, specify the page range.

 If you are deleting the page by right-clicking the thumbnail, select the **Selected** option.

5. In the **Delete Pages** dialog box, click **OK.**

6. In the **Adobe Acrobat** message box, click **OK.**

7. If necessary, scroll down the PDF document to verify that the pages you had specified have been deleted.

8. Save the PDF document.

Procedure Reference: Rearrange Pages Using the Page Thumbnails Panel

To rearrange pages using the **Page Thumbnails** panel:

1. Open the PDF document in which you want to rearrange the pages.

2. In the **Navigation Pane,** click the **Page Thumbnails** button to display the **Page Thumbnails** panel.

3. Rearrange the pages using the page thumbnails.

    ● Click and drag a page thumbnail to the desired location to move a page to a different location within the document.

    ● Hold down **Ctrl** when you drag a page thumbnail to a new location to create a copy of that page within the document.

4. Save the documents.

Procedure Reference: Customize the Page Numbering for a PDF Document

To customize the page numbering for a PDF document:

1. In the **Navigation Pane,** click the **Page Thumbnails** button and from the **Options** drop-down menu, choose **Number Pages.**

2. In the **Page Numbering** dialog box, in the **Pages** section, specify the range of pages for which the numbering needs to be modified.

3. In the **Numbering** section, specify the numbering sequence.

    ● Select the **Begin new section** option to start a new numbering sequence for the specified range of pages and specify the desired settings.

        a. From the **Style** drop-down list, select the desired style.

        b. In the **Prefix** text box, type the desired prefix.

        c. If necessary, in the **Start** text box, type the desired starting number.

    ● Select the **Extend numbering used in preceding section to selected pages** option to extend the numbering used for the pages preceding the selected pages.

4. In the **Page Numbering** dialog box, click **OK.**

5. If necessary, on the Page Navigation toolbar, in the Current Page text box, type a page number to navigate to a page based on its location.

6. Save the PDF document with the revised page numbering.

Procedure Reference: Split a PDF Document into Multiple PDF Files

To split a single PDF document into multiple PDF files:

1. Open the PDF document you want to split.

2. In the **Tools** panel, in the **Pages** section, click **Split Document.**

3. In the **Split Document** dialog box, specify the desired settings.

    ● Select the **Number of pages** option and in the **Max pages** text box, specify the number of pages you want to have in the split documents or;

    ● Select the **File size** option and specify the size for the split documents or;

    ● Select the **Top-level bookmarks** option to include bookmarks from the main document.

4. If necessary, click the **Output Options** button, specify additional settings for converting the PDF into multiple documents, and click **OK.**

5. If necessary, in the **Split Document** dialog box, click the **Apply to Multiple** button to add the desired files and click **OK** to split them into multiple PDF documents.

6. In the **Split Document** dialog box, click **OK** to split the document.

Procedure Reference: Crop Pages Using the Crop Tool

To crop pages using the **Crop** tool:

1. Crop pages and set margins in a PDF document using the **Crop** tool.

    ● In the **Tools** panel, in the **Pages** section, click **Crop** or;

    ● In the **Navigation Pane,** click the **Page Thumbnails** button and from the **Options** drop-down menu, choose **Crop.**

2. Draw a rectangle on the area of the page that has to be cropped.

3. Double-click the rectangle to display the **Set Page Boxes** dialog box and specify the desired settings.

4. Click **OK** to apply the settings for cropping a page.

5. Scroll down the PDF document to verify that the page is cropped per the specified settings.

Settings in the Crop Pages Dialog Box

The **Crop Pages** dialog box allows you to specify settings to crop pages in a PDF document.

Section	Allows You To
Crop Margins	Select the unit and pattern that has to be applied to the margins.
Margin Controls	Adjust the dimensions of the margins and remove white margins.
Change Page Size	Customize the size of a page in terms of width and height.
Page Range	Specify the range of pages that has to be cropped.

ACTIVITY 4-1
Manipulating PDF Document Pages

Data Files:

C:\084548Data\Updating PDF Documents\Employee Benefits.pdf, C:\084548Data\Updating PDF Documents\CEO Welcome.pdf

Scenario:

You want to update the Employee Benefits guide with the CEO's welcome note. When you generated the PDF version of the guide, a blank page was added to the end of the file. You want to remove that blank page.

1. Insert the CEO's welcome note as the second page in the Employee Benefits guide.

    a. From the C:\084548Data\Updating PDF Documents folder, open the Employee Benefits.pdf file.

    b. In the **Tools** panel, in the **Pages** section, in the **Insert Pages** section, click **Insert from File.**

    c. In the **Select File To Insert** dialog box, select the **CEO Welcome.pdf** file and click **Select.**

    d. In the **Insert Pages** dialog box, in the **Location** drop-down list, verify that **After** is selected.

    e. In the **Page** section, select the **First** option and click **OK.**

    f. Navigate to page 2 to view the inserted page.

    g. Save the file.

2. Remove the blank page at the end of the Employee Benefits guide.

    a. Click the **Page Thumbnails** button to display the **Page Thumbnails** panel.

    b. Scroll down and select the thumbnail of page 10 to view the page in the document pane.

    c. In the **Page Thumbnails** panel, from the **Options** drop-down menu, choose **Delete Pages.**

    d. In the **Delete Pages** dialog box, verify that the **Selected** option is selected and click **OK.**

    e. In the **Adobe Acrobat** message box, click **OK.**

3. Add page numbers to the document.

    a. Navigate to page 2.

    b. In the **Tools** panel, scroll down, in the **Edit Page Design** section, from the **Header & Footer** drop-down menu, choose **Add Header & Footer.**

c. In the **Add Header and Footer** dialog box, click in the **Right Footer Text** text box and click **Insert Page Number.**

Right Footer Text

d. In the **Right Footer Text** text box, triple-click to select the text and type *ii*

e. In the **Preview** section, click the **Page Range Options** link and in the **Page Range Options** dialog box, select the **Pages from** option and in the first text box, triple-click, type *2* and then press **Tab.**

f. In the **to** text box, type *2* and click **OK.**

g. In the **Add Header and Footer** dialog box, click **OK.**

h. Scroll down, set the zoom percentage of the document to 75, and scroll to the right to view the page number.

i. Observe that the page number appears as ii.

j. Navigate to page 3.

k. In the **Tools** panel, in the **Edit Page Design** section, from the **Header & Footer** drop-down menu, choose **Add Header & Footer.**

l. In the **Adobe Acrobat** message box, click **Add New.**

m. In the **Add Header and Footer** dialog box, click in the **Right Footer Text** text box and click **Insert Page Number.**

n. In the **Right Footer Text** text box, triple-click and type *iii*

o. In the **Preview** section, click the **Page Range Options** link and in the **Page Range Options** dialog box, select the **Pages from** option and in the first text box, triple-click, type *3* and then press **Tab.**

p. In the **to** text box, type *3* and click **OK.**

q. In the **Add Header and Footer** dialog box, click **OK.**

r. Navigate to page 4.

s. In the **Tools** panel, in the **Edit Page Design** section, from the **Header & Footer** drop-down menu, choose **Add Header & Footer.**

t. In the **Adobe Acrobat** message box, click **Add New.**

u. In the **Add Header and Footer** dialog box, click in the **Right Footer Text** text box and click **Insert Page Number.**

v. In the **Right Footer Text** text box, triple-click and type *1*

w. In the **Preview** section, click the **Page Range Options** link and in the **Page Range Options** dialog box, select the **Pages from** option and in the first and **to** text boxes, type *4*

x. Click **OK.**

y. In the **Add Header and Footer** dialog box, click **OK.**

z. Scroll down the page and scroll to the right to view the page number.

aa.   Observe that the page number appears as 1.

ab.   Similarly, add page numbers for the rest of the pages.

4.   Customize Acrobat's page numbering to match the numbering on the contents page of the document.

a.   In the **Page Thumbnails** panel, from the **Options** drop-down menu, choose **Number Pages.**

b.   In the **Page Numbering** dialog box, in the **Pages** section, verify that the **From** option is selected and in the **From** text box, double-click and type *4*

c.   In the **To** text box, type *9*

d.   In the **Numbering** section, verify that the **Begin new section** option is selected.

e.   From the **Style** drop-down list, verify that **1, 2, 3** is selected and click **OK.**

f.   In the **Navigation Pane,** scroll up, and observe that the thumbnails identify the first three pages as **1, 2,** and **3** and a new sequence begins from the fourth page. The new sequence is numbered starting from **1.**

g.   In the **Page Thumbnails** panel, scroll up to view the thumbnails of the first few pages.

h.   Observe that the thumbnails identify the first three pages as **1, 2,** and **3** and a new sequence begins from the fourth page. The new sequence is numbered starting from **1.**

5.   Change the sequence of page numbers.

a.   Navigate to page 1.

b.   In the **Page Thumbnails** panel, from the **Options** drop-down menu, choose **Number Pages.**

c.   In the **Page Numbering** dialog box, in the **Pages** section, select the **From** option and in the **From** text box, double-click and type *1*

d.   Press **Tab** and in the **To** text box, type *3*

e.   In the **Numbering** section, from the **Style** drop-down list, select **i, ii, iii** and click **OK.**

f.   Observe that the thumbnails for the first three pages display the page number in the Roman letter format.

g.   Save the file as ***My Employee Benefits*** in the PDF format.

TOPIC B
Edit Content in a PDF Document

You can now add, rearrange, and remove pages from a PDF document. After modifying the pages in the PDF document, you may find that the facts or figures used in the document have changed, necessitating a change of content. In this topic, you will edit content in a PDF document.

Editing content directly in a PDF document allows you to make changes without re-creating the PDF using the authoring application. This would save time when a document requires minimum editing that does not necessitate re-creation of the PDF document. However, if extensive changes are required to the PDF document, it is preferable to make changes in the original authoring application and re-create the PDF.

The Content Panel

The **Content** panel contains a number of options that can be used to edit content, or include media objects or bookmarks in a PDF document.

Option	Allows You To
Add Bookmark	Create a bookmark that helps in navigating to a destination in a PDF document. A destination is the end of a link, and created destinations are displayed in the **Destinations** panel. Linking to a destination is preferable when linking across documents because compared to a link to a page, a link to a destination is not affected by the addition or deletion of pages. However, this feature allows you to create destinations only if the security settings of the document permit it.
Attach a File	Attach or embed a file in a PDF. This option allows you to include large documents or files within a PDF as additional reference.
Edit Document Text	Edit text in a PDF document, provided the fonts are available in the system. If the fonts are not available, only the appearance of text can be changed. You can also add new blocks of text.
Edit Object	Modify the size, page location, and properties of images, links, fields, and multimedia objects.
Link	Create or add links to a page in the current PDF document, in another PDF document, or on a web page. You can navigate to the required destination by clicking the link.
Button	Create a button at the desired location in a PDF document. You can customize the button according to the requirement.
Multimedia	Embed or add movie, audio, AutoCAD, Flash, or other media files in a PDF document.
Select Object	Select a page in a PDF document.

The Edit Document Text Tool

You can use the **Edit Document Text** tool to delete or copy content in a PDF document. When you select this tool, a bounding box surrounding the selected text appears in the document pane. By clicking within the bounding box, the text can be modified. By right-clicking within the bounding box, you can choose the **Properties** command which allows you to modify the touchup attributes of the PDF document.

The Typewriter Toolbar

You can use the **Typewriter** toolbar for making minor edits in a PDF document. This toolbar can be displayed by clicking the **Add or Edit Text Box** tool in the **Content** panel. Using the options on the toolbar, you can change the font, font size, and apply color to text using this toolbar.

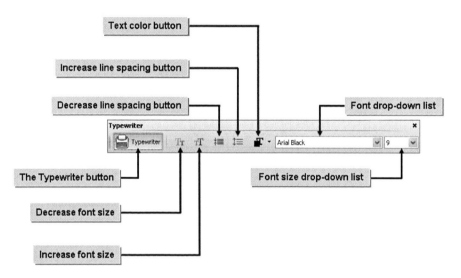

Figure 4-4: Components of the Typewriter toolbar.

Option	Used To
Font drop-down list	Change the font of the text.
Font size drop-down list	Change the font size of the text.
The **Typewriter** button	Type text in a PDF document.
Decrease font size button	Reduce the size of the text.
Increase font size button	Increase the size of the text.
Decrease line spacing button	Reduce the line spacing of the text.
Increase line spacing button	Increase the line spacing of the text.
Text Color button	Change the color of the text.

Limitations in Using the Typewriter Toolbar

A PDF file is intended to closely reflect the content of the file from which it was created. For minor edits, you can use the **TouchUp Text** tool. However, there are certain limitations to editing text in a PDF document. To make extensive changes to the document, you should open the file in the authoring application, modify the contents, and re-create the PDF.

Limitation	Description
No text wrapping	In a PDF document, each line of text is treated as a separate object. So, adding text within a line in a paragraph will not cause the text at the end of the line to flow to the next line.
Embedding text	The font for the text you edit should be either installed on your computer or embedded in the document. Otherwise, the font will appear different while printing or viewing the PDF.

How to Edit Content in a PDF Document

Procedure Reference: Edit Text Using the Options in the Content Panel

To edit text using the options in the **Content** panel:

1. In the **Content** panel, in the **Edit Text & Objects** section, select the **Edit Document Text** tool.

2. In the document pane, select the text you want to edit to display it within a bounding box.

3. Within the bounding box, select the text you want to edit.

   - Choose **Edit→Select All** to select the entire text within the bounding box or;
   - Click and drag to select a portion of text to be edited or;
   - Choose **Edit→Delete** to delete the text or;
   - Choose **Edit→Copy** to copy the selected text.

4. Click outside the box to deselect the editing area.

5. If necessary, add new text to the document.

   a. Hold down **Ctrl** and click in the document where you want to add text.

   b. In the **New Text Font** dialog box, specify the options to select the text font and writing mode, and click **OK.**

   c. Type the text and click outside the text block to deselect the text.

Procedure Reference: Edit Text Attributes Using the Edit Document Text Toolbar

To edit text attributes using the **Edit Document Text** toolbar:

1. In the **Tools** panel, in the **Content** section, in the **Edit Text & Objects** section, click **Edit Document Text.**

2. Select the text for which the attributes need to be changed.

3. Within the bounding box that is displayed, select the text to be changed, right-click, and choose **Properties.**

4. In the **TouchUp Properties** dialog box, change the desired text attributes and click **Close.**

 Baseline refers to the line on which the type rests. The **Baseline Offset** option is available on the **Text** tab in the **TouchUp Properties** dialog box using which you can change the line spacing in a PDF document.

Procedure Reference: Insert Text Using the Typewriter Toolbar

To insert text using the **Typewriter** toolbar:

1. Open the PDF document in which you want to insert text.
2. In the **Content** panel, in the **Edit Text & Objects** section, click **Add or Edit Text Box** to display the **Typewriter** toolbar.
3. Click in the location where you want to include the text and type the text.
4. Click the **Text Color** button to change the color of the font and click outside the type-written text to deselect it.
5. Save the PDF document.

Procedure Reference: Edit Images Using the Edit Object Toolbar

To edit images using the **Edit Object** toolbar:

1. If necessary, specify the image editor.
   a. Choose **Edit→Preferences.**
   b. In the **Preferences** dialog box, in the **Categories** list box, scroll down and select **TouchUp** to display the touchup preferences settings in the right pane.
   c. In the **Image Editor** section, click **Choose Image Editor.**
   d. In the **Choose Image Editor** dialog box, navigate to and select the image editor you want to use to edit the image.
   e. Click **Open** to assign the image editing program to the function.
   f. Click **OK.**
2. In the **Tools** panel, in the **Content** section, in the **Edit Text & Objects** section, click **Edit Object.**
3. Using the **Edit Object** tool, click the image to display a bounding box around it.
4. Right-click the image and choose **Edit Image** to display the selected image in the image editing application.
5. In the **TouchUp** message box, click **Yes.**
6. Make the necessary changes to the image.
7. Save the image and close the application.
8. Save the PDF document.

ACTIVITY 4-2
Editing Text in the 2010-2011 Benefits Changes Guide

Data Files:

C:\084548Data\Updating PDF Documents\My Employee Benefits.pdf , C:\084548Data\ Updating PDF Documents\2010-2011 Benefits Change.pdf

Before You Begin:

The My Employee Benefits.pdf file is open.

Scenario:

You received the 2010–2011 Benefits Changes.pdf document. You review the file before distributing it to the employees. You find that the pages are not numbered properly. Because the document contains only four pages, you decide to update the page numbers manually. The first page of the document contains a chart and a table describing the maternity and paternity leave policy. You want to add a title to the chart and plan to crop empty areas on all the pages to render a compact structure to the entire document.

1. Title the chart as *Extended Maternity/Paternity Leave.*

    a. From the C:\084548Data\Updating PDF Documents folder, open the 2010–2011 Benefits Change.pdf file.

    b. Select the **Tools** panel, select the **Content** section, and in the **Edit Text & Objects** section, click **Edit Object.**

    c. On page 1, select the chart image.

    d. In the **Edit Text & Objects** section, click **Add or Edit Text Box** to display the **Typewriter** toolbar.

    e. Hold down **Ctrl** and click above the chart.

    f. On the **Typewriter** toolbar, from the **Font** drop-down list, select **Times Roman.**

    g. Type *Extended Maternity/Paternity Leave*

2. Add page numbers to the document.

    a. Scroll down to view the table below the bar graph on page 1.

    b. Hold down **Ctrl** and click at the bottom-right corner of the page.

    c. On the **Typewriter** toolbar, from the **Font** drop-down list, select **Arial.**

    d. At the bottom-right corner of the page, type *1*

    e. Scroll down to the next page.

    f. In page 2, click at the bottom-left corner of the page and type *2*

    g. Similarly, add page numbers for pages 3 and 4.

    h. Click **Typewriter** to close the **Typewriter** toolbar.

        i.   Select the Selection tool and click in the blank space below the text to deselect the selected text.

3.   Crop empty areas on pages 2–4 of the document.

        a.   In the **Tools** panel, expand the **Pages** section, and click **Crop.**

        b.   Double-click in the document pane to display the **Set Page Boxes** dialog box.

        c.   In the **Set Page Boxes** dialog box, in the **Margin Controls** section, check the **Remove White Margins** check box.

        d.   In the **Page Range** section, verify that the **From** option is selected.

        e.   In the **From** text box, double-click, specify the value as *2* and then click **OK.**

        f.   Save the file as *My 2010-2011 Benefits Change* in the PDF format and close the file.

TOPIC C
Add Page Elements

You familiarized yourself with editing content in a PDF document. You may now need to add extra information to make the document more detailed without increasing the page count. In this topic, you will add customized page elements to a PDF document.

After editing content in a PDF document, you may want to include additional information that would help identify the document's author or status. You may also want to add visual interest to your document to make it more engaging for the reader. Using page elements such as headers, footers, watermarks, and backgrounds, you can make your document look visually appealing and attractive.

Headers and Footers

Headers and footers are used to present information at the top and bottom margins of a document, respectively. Common header and footer information includes the title of a document, page number, author name, and date. You can also add headers and footers to a PDF portfolio. You can add a header that displays the page number on the right side of odd pages and another header that displays the page number on the left side of even pages.

Watermarks and Backgrounds

Watermarks and backgrounds are either graphic or text elements added to document pages. Watermarks overlap document content, while backgrounds appear behind the content. Watermarks and backgrounds can be placed on all pages or a range of pages. The font color, opacity, and rotation degree of the text used in watermarks can also be adjusted.

How to Add Page Elements

Procedure Reference: Add Headers and Footers to a PDF Document

To add headers and footers to a PDF document:

1. In the **Tools** panel, in the **Pages** section, click **Header & Footer.**
2. In the **Add Header and Footer** dialog box, click in the header or footer text boxes and specify the appropriate header or footer information.
3. If necessary, in the **Font** section, modify the font type and font size of the header or footer attributes.
4. If necessary, in the **Margin (Inches)** section, specify values in the **Top, Bottom, Left,** and **Right** text boxes to define the distance between the page edges and the header or the footer.
5. If necessary, click the **Appearance Options** link to display the **Appearance Options** dialog box, specify the settings for streamlining the appearance of headers and footers, and click **OK.**

6. If necessary, specify the page number and date format settings for automatic entries.

    a. Click the **Page Number and Date Format** link.

    b. In the **Page Number and Date Format** dialog box, specify the formats for automatic date and page number entries.

    c. If necessary, specify the start page number.

    d. Click **OK.**

7. If necessary, in the **Add Header and Footer** dialog box, click one of the header or footer text boxes, and click the **Insert Date** or **Insert Page Number** button to enable automatic date or page number entries.

8. If necessary, click the **Page Range Options** link to display the **Page Range Options** dialog box and then specify the page range for the header and footer to appear and click **OK.**

    - Select the **All Pages** option to add headers and footers to all pages.

    - Specify a number in the **Pages From** and **To** text boxes to display the header or footer only on specific pages.

    - From the **Subset** drop-down list, select the desired option to restrict the header and footer in a document to specific pages.

9. If necessary, in the **Preview** section, preview the header or footer to verify that it is displayed as required.

10. Click **OK.**

Procedure Reference: Add Watermarks to a PDF Document

To add watermarks to a PDF document:

1. In the **Tools** panel, in the **Pages** section, in the **Watermark** section, click **Add Watermark.**

2. In the **Add Watermark** dialog box, in the **Source** section, specify the watermark you want to use.

    - Select **Text** and, in the text box to its right, type the text you want to use and then specify the font, size, color, and alignment of the text to display text as a watermark.

    - Select **File,** click **Browse,** navigate to and select the image file you want to add, and click **Open.** If the watermark is in a multiple page document, then in the **Page Number** text box, specify the page number containing the watermark to add an image as a watermark.

3. In the **Appearance** section, specify options to modify the appearance of the watermark.

    - In the **Rotation** text box, specify a value to set an angle of rotation for the watermark.

    - Drag the **Opacity** slider, or type a value in the **Opacity** text box to specify the degree of opacity of the watermark.

    - Click the **Appearance Options** link, check the desired check boxes, and click **OK.**

4. If necessary, in the **Position** section, set the vertical and horizontal positions of the watermark on the document pages, and specify the required alignment value.

5. If necessary, resize the watermark.

   • In the **Source** section, in the **Absolute Scale** spin box, specify a percentage to resize the watermark in relation to the actual size of the original image file.

   • In the **Appearance** section, check the **Scale Relative To Target Page** check box and then select a percentage from the spin box on the right to resize the watermark in relation to the PDF page dimensions.

6. If necessary, click the **Page Range Options** link, specify the pages on which you want the watermark to be visible, and click **OK.**

7. In the **Add Watermark** dialog box, click **OK.**

Procedure Reference: Add Backgrounds to a PDF Document

To add backgrounds to a PDF document:

1. In the **Tools** panel, in the **Pages** section, in the **Background** section, click **Add Background.**

2. In the **Add Background** dialog box, in the **Source** section, specify the background type.

   • Select **From color,** click the box to its right, and select the desired color to apply as the background color.

   • Select **File,** click **Browse,** navigate to and select the image file you want to add, and click **Open.** If the background is in a multiple page document, then in the **Page Number** text box, specify the page number containing the background.

 Only PDF, JPEG, and BMP files can be used as background images.

3. In the **Appearance** section, specify the appearance of the background.

   • In the **Rotation** spin box, specify a value to set an angle of rotation for the background.

   • Drag the **Opacity** slider, or type a value in the **Opacity** text box, to specify the degree of opacity of the background.

   • Click the **Appearance Options** link, check the desired check boxes, and click **OK.**

4. If necessary, set the vertical and horizontal positions of the background on the document pages and specify the required alignment value.

5. If necessary, resize the background.

   • In the **Source** section, in the **Absolute Scale** spin box, specify a percentage to resize the image to the specified percentage of its full-size display.

   • In the **Appearance** section, check the **Scale Relative to Target Page** check box and then select a percentage from the spin box on the right, to resize the background in relation to the PDF page dimensions.

6. If necessary, click the **Page Range Options** link, specify the pages on which you want the background to be visible, and click **OK.**

7. In the **Add Background** dialog box, click **OK.**

ACTIVITY 4-3
Adding Headers and Footers to the Benefits Guide

Before You Begin:
The My Employee Benefits.pdf file is open.

Scenario:
While preparing the new Employee Benefits document, you realize that many employees will print the document and put the pages in a binder, along with other materials relating to employment benefits. You decide to present the document in such a way that they can easily distinguish the pages of the Benefits guide from those of other documents.

1. Add a header to the Employee Benefits.pdf document.

   a. In the **Tools** panel, in the **Pages** section, in the **Edit Page Design** section, from the **Header & Footer** drop-down menu, choose **Add Header & Footer.**

   b. In the **Adobe Acrobat** message box, click **Add New.**

   c. In the **Add Header and Footer** dialog box, click in the **Center Header Text** text box and type *Rudison Employee Benefits*

   d. In the **Font** section, from the **Name** drop-down list, select **Arial Bold.**

   e. From the **Size** drop-down list, select **9.**

   f. Click the **Appearance Options** link.

   g. In the **Appearance Options** dialog box, check the **Keep position and size of header/footer text constant when printing on different page sizes** check box and click **OK.**

2. Set the header to display 0.17 inch below the top edge of the page on pages 4 through 8.

   a. Click the **Page Range Options** link.

   b. In the **Page Range Options** dialog box, select the **Pages from** option and in the first text box, triple-click and type *4*

   c. In the **to** text box, verify that **8** is displayed.

   d. Click **OK** to close the **Page Range Options** dialog box.

   e. In the **Margins (Inches)** section, in the **Top** text box, triple-click to select the displayed value, type *0.17* and click **OK** to apply the settings.

   f. Scroll down to page ii and observe that the page does not contain a header.

   g. Scroll down to page 1 and observe that the header "Rudison Employee Benefits" is displayed. Save the file.

ACTIVITY 4-4
Adding a Watermark to the Employee Benefits Guide

Before You Begin:
The My Employee Benefits.pdf file is open.

Scenario:
The header of the Benefits document is not easily distinguishable from other documents. So, you want to add page elements that will help you differentiate this document just by looking at it.

1. Add a watermark to pages 4 through 8.

   a. In the **Tools** panel, in the **Pages** section, in the **Edit Page Design** section, from the **Watermark** drop-down menu, choose **Add Watermark.**

   b. In the **Add Watermark** dialog box, in the **Source** section, in the text box to the right of the **Text** option, click and type *Sample*

   c. In the **Appearance** section, select the **45°** option.

   d. Verify that the **Appear on top of page** option is selected.

   e. In the **Opacity** text box, triple-click, type *25* and then press **Enter.**

   f. At the top right of the dialog box, click the **Page Range Options** link.

   g. In the **Page Range Options** dialog box, select the **Pages from** option to specify the pages on which you want the watermark to be visible.

   h. Triple-click in the **Pages from** text box and type *4*

   i. Verify that in the **to** text box, **8** is displayed and then click **OK** to close the **Page Range Options** dialog box.

   j. In the **Add Watermark** dialog box, click **OK** to apply the settings.

   k. In the document pane, scroll down the page to view the watermark.

   l. Observe the Sample watermark.

2. Add a light gray background to all pages in the Benefits document.

   a. In the **Tools** panel, in the **Pages** section, in the **Edit Page Design** section, from the **Background** drop-down menu, choose **Add Background.**

   b. In the **Add Background** dialog box, in the **Source** section, verify that the **From color** option is selected.

   c. Click the box to the right of the **From color** option to display the color palette.

   d. In the fourth row, last column, select the light gray shade.

   e. In the **Appearance** section, triple-click in the **Opacity** text box, type *25* and then press **Enter.**

       f.   At the top right of the dialog box, click the **Page Range Options** link.

       g.   In the **Page Range Options** dialog box, verify that the **All Pages** option is selected.

       h.   Click **OK** to close the **Page Range Options** dialog box.

       i.   In the **Add Background** dialog box, click **OK** to apply the settings.

       j.   Save the file.

TOPIC D

Extract Content from a PDF Document

You created and edited a PDF document. Now, you may need to reuse some of its content in some other authoring application. In this topic, you will extract text and images from a PDF document.

Extracting content directly from a PDF document and including it in a new file helps ensure that the desired PDF content is accurately reproduced elsewhere.

Image Formats for Extracting

Acrobat allows you to save images from PDF files that can be included in other applications or programs. This helps you to retain the fidelity of the reused content. You can save an image present in a PDF file as a JPEG, TIFF, or Bitmap file.

The Extract Pages Dialog Box

The **Extract Pages** dialog box allows you to extract specific pages from a PDF document for reuse. Using the Selection tool, you can export specific content from PDF documents to other formats such as Microsoft Word. This enables you to retain the accuracy of the reused content. You can copy a paragraph or selected text from a PDF file, export, and save it as a Microsoft Word document.

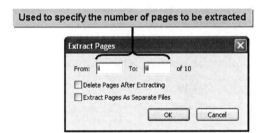

Figure 4-5: Options available in the Extract Pages dialog box.

How to Extract Content from a PDF Document

Procedure Reference: Extract Pages from a PDF Document

To extract pages from a PDF document:

1. In Acrobat X Pro, open the document containing the pages you want to extract.

2. Display the **Extract Pages** dialog box.

   - In the **Tools** panel, select the **Pages** section and click **Extract.**

   - In the **Navigation Pane,** click the **Page Thumbnails** button and from the **Options** drop-down menu, choose **Extract Pages.**

3. In the **Extract Pages** dialog box, in the **From** and **To** text boxes, specify the range of pages to be extracted.

4. If necessary, in the **Extract Pages** dialog box, specify additional settings for extracting the pages.

   - Check the **Delete Pages After Extracting** check box to remove pages from the original document after extracting them.

   - Check the **Extract Pages As Separate Files** check box to convert each extracted page as a separate PDF file.

5. In the **Extract Pages** dialog box, click **OK** to apply the page extraction settings.

6. In the **Adobe Acrobat** message box, click **Yes** to confirm the deletion.

7. Save the new file.

Procedure Reference: Copy Content for Use in Other Applications

To copy content for use in other applications:

1. Select the PDF content you want to use in another application.

   a. On the **Select & Zoom** toolbar, select the Selection tool.

   b. Click at the beginning of the section from which you want to copy the content.

   c. Hold down **Shift** and click at the end of the section up to the location you want to copy.

2. Move the selected content to the desired location.

   - Choose **Edit→Copy** to copy the content and then paste it in the desired application or;

   - Click and drag the content to another application's open document window and place it in the desired location.

 When you use the copied content from a PDF document for use in other applications, only the text is copied. In order to copy images, you have to select the images individually and copy them, or you can export all the images from a PDF document.

 After selecting content, if the **Cut** and **Copy** commands are disabled, the PDF document's author may have specified settings to restrict readers from copying the document's content.

Procedure Reference: Save Copied Text in a Microsoft Word Document

To save copied text in a Microsoft Word document:

1. Select and copy the PDF document content you want to use in Microsoft Word.
2. Choose **Start→All Programs→Microsoft Office→Microsoft Word 2010.**
3. On the **Home** tab, in the **Clipboard** group, click **Paste.**
4. Choose **File→Save As→Word Document.**
5. In the **Save As** dialog box, navigate to the desired folder and save the file with a new name.

Procedure Reference: Save Images from a PDF Document in an Image Format

To copy images for use in other applications:

1. Open the PDF document that has the required image.
2. On the **Select & Zoom** toolbar, select the Selection tool.
3. Click the image to select it.
4. Right-click the selected image and choose **Save Image As** to display the **Save Image As** dialog box.
5. If necessary, in the **Save Image As** dialog box, navigate to the desired location where you want to save the file.
6. If necessary, in the **File name** text box, type a new name for the file.
7. If necessary, from the **Save as type** drop-down list, select the desired file format in which you want to save the file.
8. Click **Save.**

Procedure Reference: Convert a PDF Document to Other File Formats

To convert a PDF document to other file formats:

1. Choose **File→Save As.**
2. In the **Save As** dialog box, from the type drop-down list, select the desired text or image format.
3. If necessary, click **Settings** to display the **Save As *[File Format]* Settings** dialog box. Specify the desired options and click **OK.**
4. If necessary, in the **Save As** dialog box, in the **File name** text box, type a new name for the file.
5. Navigate to a specific location and click **Save** to save the PDF document in the specified format.
6. If necessary, open the converted document to verify that it is saved in the format you specified.

 The generated document's appearance may not match the appearance of the PDF document.

Procedure Reference: Export Images from a PDF Document

To export images from a PDF document:

1. In the **Tools** panel, in the **Document Processing** section, click **Export All Images** to display the **Export All Images As** dialog box.

2. If necessary, click **Settings** to display the **Export All Images As JPEG Settings** dialog box, specify additional settings for exporting the images, and click **OK.**

3. If necessary, in the **Export All Images As** dialog box, in the **File name** text box, type a new name for the file.

4. Specify the location where you want to save the images and click **Save.**

ACTIVITY 4-5
Using Text and Images from a PDF File

Scenario:
The previous version of the Employee Benefits guide included a staff list. You decide to use the list as a separate document for reference. You are also asked to make a list of the holidays and the leave policy of Rudison Technologies. You need to reuse content from the available benefits guide. You want to copy relevant images and include them in the leave policy document. This will help you to retain the basic format of the document, while sharing new information with other employees.

1. Extract page 6 as a separate document from the My Employee Benefits.pdf file.

   a. In the **Navigation Pane,** click the **Page Thumbnails** button to display the **Page Thumbnails** panel.

   b. In the **Page Thumbnails** panel, right-click the page 6 thumbnail and choose **Extract Pages.**

   c. In the **Extract Pages** dialog box, verify that in the **From** and **To** text boxes **6** is displayed and click **OK.**

   d. Observe that the extracted page is displayed as Pages from My Employee Benefits.pdf document.

   e. Choose **File→Save As→PDF.**

   f. If necessary, in the **Save As** dialog box, navigate to the C:\084548Data\Updating PDF Documents folder.

   g. In the **Save As** dialog box, in the **File name** text box, type *Staff List* and click **Save.**

   h. Close the Staff List.pdf file.

2. Copy the leave policy from the "Holidays & Leave" page of the Benefits guide.

   a. Navigate to page 3.

   b. Set the zoom percentage to 75.

   c. Scroll down, under the sub-heading "Personal/Sick Leave," in the second paragraph, click before the word "There" and scroll to right. Hold down **Shift** and click after the word "schedule" at the end of the paragraph.

   d. Choose **Edit→Copy** to copy the selected text.

3. Save the list in a Microsoft Word document.

   a. Choose **Start→All Programs→Microsoft Word 2010.**

   b. On the **Home** tab, in the **Clipboard** group, click **Paste.**

   c. Select the **File** tab and choose **Save As.**

    d.   In the **Save As** dialog box, navigate to the C:\084548Data\Updating PDF Documents folder.

    e.   In the **Save As** dialog box, in the **File name** text box, select the text, type *Leave Policy* and then click **Save.**

    f.   Close the Microsoft Word application.

4.   Save the ship image on the "Holidays & Leave" page of the Benefits guide as a BMP file.

    a.   In the document pane, scroll up to select the ship image.

    b.   Right-click the selected image and choose **Save Image As.**

    c.   In the **Save Image As** dialog box, in the **File name** text box, type *Ship Image*

    d.   In the **Save as type** drop-down list, verify that **Bitmap Image Files (*.bmp)** is selected and click **Save.**

    e.   Close the My Employee Benefits.pdf file.

Lesson 4 Follow-up

In this lesson, you modified a PDF document by arranging pages, editing content, adding headers and footers, and customizing page numbers. Being able to modify PDF pages within Acrobat enables you to display the information required in the desired order, without having to re-create the PDF using the original authoring application.

1. **After creating a PDF document, what types of modifications do you expect to make?**

2. **What techniques are most useful for modifying PDF documents? Why?**

5 | Working with Multiple PDF Documents

Lesson Time: 30 minutes

Lesson Objectives:

In this lesson, you will work with multiple PDF documents.

You will:

- Control access to multiple PDF documents.

- Search multiple PDF documents.

Introduction

You updated individual PDF documents. Sometimes, you may need to view or update several related PDF documents. In this lesson, you will work with multiple PDF documents.

At work, you may have to deal with multiple documents that need password protection to secure confidential information, and use the search options to locate certain words and phrases available in the current PDF document or across multiple documents. Using Acrobat, you will be able to efficiently work with multiple PDF documents.

TOPIC A
Control Access to Multiple PDF Documents

You updated PDF documents. After updating the PDF documents, you will need to control access to those documents. In this topic, you will control user access to multiple PDF documents.

You may have created several PDF documents and distributed them to users. You may want a few members to review the PDF documents and modify them, while the others would just view them. You would also like to secure the document so that it is not tampered by others. By controlling access to PDF documents, you can determine how recipients use each PDF document.

Document Security Options

There are several options available to enhance security when creating Adobe PDF documents.

Security Option	Enables You To
No Security	Disable security settings.
Password Security	Add passwords and set security options to restrict opening, editing, and printing of PDF documents. A PDF can have two types of passwords: a document open password and a change permissions password. The document open password requires the user to specify the password to open the document; the change permissions password, to specify the password for modifying the document.
Certificate Security	Encrypt a document so that only a specified set of users can have access to it.
Adobe LiveCycle Rights Management	Apply server-based security policies to PDF documents. Server-based security policies are useful if you want others to have access to PDF documents only for a limited time.

 If the same security settings are used for a set of PDF documents, you can create a security policy to simplify your workflow.

The Remove Hidden Information Option

You can find and remove additional content such as metadata, bookmarks, file attachments, and hidden text in a PDF document using the **Remove Hidden Information** feature. Each of these content types is displayed along with the number of occurrences in the **Remove Hidden Information** panel. You can specify the content type you want to examine by checking the appropriate check box and then use the **Remove** button to remove the selected content. This feature ensures that the PDF provides only the content that the author intends to share with others.

Redaction

Redaction allows you to permanently remove or redact specific text or images from a PDF document. It is generally used to hide sensitive information. You can use the commands present in the **Black Out & Remove Content** section to redact the desired information.

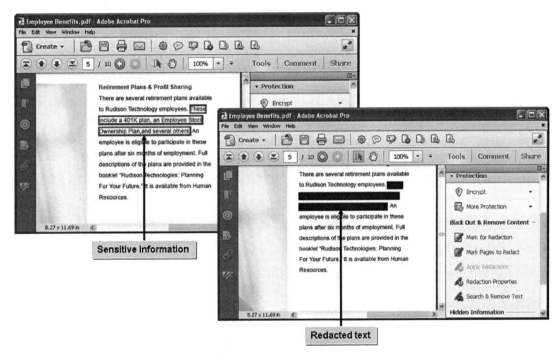

Figure 5-1: PDF document with redacted text.

Auto-Append File Name

Each time a document is saved after applying redactions, Acrobat prompts the user to auto-append the file name. Choosing a new name for your document will enable you to have one copy without redaction and another copy with redactions applied.

Redaction Options

There are five redaction tools for redacting content from a document.

Redaction Tool	Allows You To
Mark for Redaction	Select the text to be redacted by pointing over it using the insertion point. You can select an image or an image together with text by drawing a rectangle over the selection. You can place the mouse pointer over the marked content to have a preview of redaction marks.
Mark Pages to Redact	Specify the current page or the page range that can be redacted.
Apply Redactions	Apply redactions to hide the text or image marked for redaction. This tool is enabled only after you have marked the content for redaction. By default, the redacted contents are filled with black color. You can change the color of the redaction marks.
Redaction Properties	Modify the redaction marks. You can specify the **Redacted Area** fill color box and the overlay text, if needed. It also allows you to change the font properties of the overlay text and its alignment. In addition, you can select either the **Custom Text** option or the **Redaction Code** option as the overlay text.
Search & Remove Text	Locate a specific word or phrase within the current document or within PDF documents in a specific folder. You can then choose to redact all or specific instances of the search term.

How to Control Access to Multiple PDF Documents

Procedure Reference: Redact Sensitive Content

To redact sensitive content:

1. Choose **View→Tools→Protection.**
2. In the **Protections** section, in the **Black Out & Remove Content** section, click **Mark for Redaction.**
3. In the **Using Redaction Tools** message box, click **OK.**
4. Select the content you want to remove.
   - Double-click to select a word or image.
   - Click and drag to select a line, a block of text, an object, or an area.
5. Click **Redaction Properties** to display the **Redaction Tool Properties** dialog box and perform the desired actions.
   - Specify the settings on the **General** tab.
     - In the **Author** text box, specify the author name.
     - In the **Subject** text box, type the subject.
   - Specify the settings on the **Appearance** tab.
     - Click the **Redacted Area Fill Color** color box and from the color palette, select a fill color to apply the desired color to the area marked for redaction.

- Check the **Use Overlay Text** check box and specify the desired settings for the overlay text.
- In the **Redaction Mark Appearance** section, click the **Outline Color** color box to select the desired color for the outline of the redacted mark.
- In the **Fill Opacity** text box, specify the value for the opacity.

6. Click **OK.**

7. In the **Black Out & Remove Content** section, click **Apply Redactions** to redact the marked items.

8. In the **Adobe Acrobat** message box, click **OK** to confirm redaction.

9. If necessary, in the **Adobe Acrobat** message box, click **No** to prevent your document from being examined for additional document information.

Procedure Reference: Redact Content Across Multiple Documents

To redact content across multiple documents:

1. In the **Protections** panel, in the **Black Out & Remove Content** section, click **Search and Remove Text.**

2. In the **Adobe Acrobat** dialog box, click **OK** to display the Search window.

3. In the **Where would you like to search** section, select **All PDF Documents in.**

4. From the **All PDF Documents in** drop-down list, select the location where you want to search for and redact a word or phrase.

5. In the **Search for** section, specify the search options.

6. In the **What word or phrase would you like to search for** text box, type the word or phrase you want to search for.

7. Click **Search and Redact.**

8. In the **Results** section, click **Check All.**

9. Click **Mark Checked Results for Redaction.**

10. In the **Output Options** dialog box, check the **Apply redaction marks** check box and click **OK.**

Procedure Reference: Restrict Access to a PDF Document

To restrict access to a PDF document:

1. Choose **File→Properties** and select the **Security** tab.

2. From the **Security Method** drop-down list, select **Password Security.**

3. In the **Password Security - Settings** dialog box, specify the password security settings.

   a. From the **Compatibility** drop-down list, select the version of Acrobat with which you want the security settings to be compatible.

    The options in the **Password Security - Settings** dialog box might vary depending on the compatibility option selected.

   b. In the **Select Document Components To Encrypt** section, specify the required settings for the document components you want to encrypt.

   - Select the **Encrypt all document contents** option to encrypt the contents of a document and restrict search engines from accessing the metadata.

- Select the **Encrypt all document contents except metadata (Acrobat 6 and later compatible)** option to encrypt the contents of a document, but allow search engines to access the metadata.

- Select the **Encrypt only file attachments (Acrobat 7 and later compatible)** option to encrypt only the file attachments.

 The settings in the **Permissions** section are unavailable for file attachments.

c. Specify a password to open the document or file attachments.

- Check the **Require a password to open the document** check box and in the **Document Open Password** text box, type a password.

- In the **File Attachment Open Password** text box, type a password.

 The **File Attachment Open Password** text box is available only if the **Encrypt only file attachments (Acrobat 7 and later compatible)** option is selected in the **Specify Documents to Encrypt** section.

d. If necessary, restrict editing and printing of the document.

- Check the **Restrict editing and printing of the document** check box and in the **Change Permissions Password** text box, specify a password.

 You cannot specify the same password used for opening the document.

- From the **Printing Allowed** drop-down list, select the document's print option.

- From the **Changes Allowed** drop-down list, select the editing actions allowed in the document.

- If necessary, at the bottom of the **Permissions** section, check both check boxes to enable copying of content and to enable text access for screen reader devices for the visually impaired.

 At the bottom of the **Permissions** section, one or more check boxes may be displayed, based on the compatibility option you select.

4. Click **OK.**

5. In the **Adobe Acrobat - Confirm Document Open Password** text box, retype the password and click **OK.**

6. In the **Adobe Acrobat** message box, click **OK.**

7. In the **Adobe Acrobat - Confirm Permissions Properties** dialog box, type the password and click **OK.**

8. In the **Adobe Acrobat** message box, click **OK.**

9. Close the **Document Properties** dialog box.

10. Save the file.

11. Close the PDF document.

Compatibility Options for a Document's Security

You can specify the type of encryption to be used on a document by selecting the appropriate compatibility option. The table below lists the compatibility options that are available in the **Password Security - Settings** dialog box.

Compatibility Option	*Description*
Acrobat 3.0 and later	This option uses a low encryption level. The file can be opened using Acrobat versions 3.0 and later.
Acrobat 5.0 and later	This option uses a high encryption level. The file cannot be opened using Acrobat versions prior to version 5.0.
Acrobat 6.0 and later	This option enables plaintext metadata for searching.
Acrobat 7.0 and later	This option enables plaintext metadata for searching and encrypts only file attachments.
Acrobat X and later	This option enables plaintext metadata for searching and encrypts only file attachments.

Procedure Reference: Remove Security Settings from a PDF Document

To remove security settings from a PDF document:

1. Choose **File→Properties** to display the **Document Properties** dialog box.
2. Select the **Security** tab and from the **Security Method** drop-down list, select **No Security.**
3. In the **Document Properties** dialog box, click **OK.**
4. Close the PDF document.

Procedure Reference: Remove Hidden Information from a Document

To remove hidden information from a document.

1. Choose **View→Tools→Protection.**
2. In the **Protection** panel, in the **Hidden Information** section, click **Remove Hidden Information** to find the hidden information in the document.
3. The hidden information will be displayed in a nested structure in the **Results** section on the left side of the document pane.

 A message box is displayed at the bottom of the panel saying, **"Acrobat has found the following hidden information. Click Remove to remove all selected items."**

4. In the **Results** section, verify that the check boxes are checked only for the items you want to remove from the document and click **Remove.**
5. In the **Remove Hidden Information** message box, click **OK.**

ACTIVITY 5-1
Controlling Access to Multiple PDF Documents

Data Files:

C:\084548Data\Working with Multiple PDF Documents\Employee Benefits.pdf

Scenario:

Several employees have requested a copy of the Employee Benefits guide. You have used the Employee Benefits.pdf file and created navigation links to new changes made to the document. Before you make these documents accessible to others, you want to remove sensitive content. Also, you want to secure certain documents so that inadvertent changes can be avoided, and printing of those documents can be prevented.

1. Redact the first two sentences in the Retirement Plans & Profit Sharing subheading.

   a. From the C:\084548Data\Working with Multiple PDF Documents folder, open the Employee Benefits.pdf file.

   b. Navigate to page 2.

   c. Choose **View→Tools→Protection.**

   d. In the **Tools** panel, in the **Protection** section, in the **Black Out & Remove Content** section, click **Mark for Redaction.**

   e. In the **Using Redaction Tools** message box, click **OK.**

   f. In the document pane, under the subheading "Retirement Plans & Profit Sharing," select the first two sentences.

   g. In the **Black Out & Remove Content** section, click **Redaction Properties.**

   h. In the **Redaction Tool Properties** dialog box, click the **Redacted Area Fill** color box to display the color palette.

   i. In the second row, last column, select the gray color on the extreme right to apply the color to the area marked for redaction and click **OK.**

   j. In the **Black Out & Remove Content** section, click **Apply Redactions** to redact the marked content.

   k. In the **Adobe Acrobat** message box, click **OK** to confirm redaction of the marked content.

   l. In the **Adobe Acrobat** message box, click **No.**

   m. Save the file as *My Employee Benefits_Redacted* in the PDF format.

2. Secure the Employee Benefits guide.

   a. Choose **File→Properties.**

   b. In the **Document Properties** dialog box, select the **Security** tab.

c.   In the **Document Security** section, from the **Security Method** drop-down list, select **Password Security.**

d.   In the **Password Security - Settings** dialog box, in the **Permissions** section, check **Restrict editing and printing of the document. A password will be required in order to change these permission settings.**

e.   In the **Change Permissions Password** text box, type ***password1234*** and click **OK.**

f.   In the **Adobe Acrobat** message box, click **OK.**

g.   In the **Adobe Acrobat - Confirm Permissions Password** dialog box, in the **Permissions Password** text box, type ***password1234*** and click **OK.**

h.   In the **Adobe Acrobat** message box, click **OK.**

i.   In the **Document Properties** dialog box, click **OK.**

j.   Save the file.

k.   On the title bar, observe that the text "(SECURED)" is displayed along with the file name.

l.   In the **Navigation Pane,** click the **Security Settings** button. 🔒

m.   In the **Security Settings** panel, observe the message, "This document has an open password or a modify password. You cannot print or copy this document."

n.   Close the My Employee Benefits_Redacted.pdf (SECURED) file.

TOPIC B
Search Multiple PDF Documents

You familiarized yourself with controlling user access to multiple PDF documents. While working on multiple documents, you may be required to locate specific contents. Searching a document manually can be cumbersome and time consuming. In this topic, you will use Acrobat to search through a group of PDF documents to locate all instances of a particular word or phrase.

Your company address has changed; so, you want to locate all instances of the address in the marketing material for changing the old address. Rather than opening each PDF document individually and risking the chance of missing occurrences of the address, you can use Acrobat to instantaneously search all PDF documents in the Marketing folder. This will ensure that you identify every instance that needs to be changed.

Metadata

Definition:

Metadata is text that concisely describes a document. It includes information about the document and its contents. Metadata is typically used to specify the title, author, subject, and keywords that can be used to enrich searching options for the document.

Example:

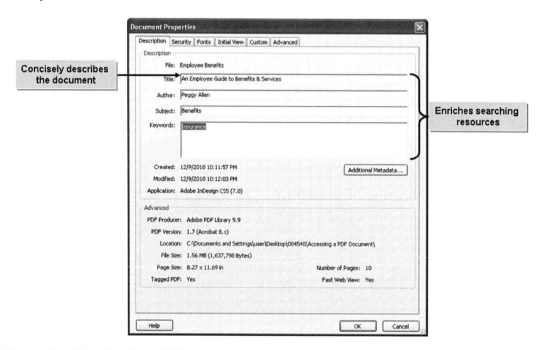

Figure 5-2: *Metadata in a PDF document.*

Advanced Search Options

You can view the advanced search options by clicking the **Show More Options** link at the bottom of the Search window. These options allow you to either broaden or restrict your search results.

Option	Used To
Match Exact word or phrase	Search for an entire string of characters including spaces.
Match Any of the words	Search for instances of at least one of the words typed, for instances that contain the complete word, for words that match the casing of the typed text, for a set of two or more words, or for the text that is part of a specified search word.
Match All of the words	Search for all instances of the text typed. This option is available only for search of multiple documents or index definition files.
Boolean query	Search for all instances of words using the "AND," "OR," "^," or "( )" operator.
Include Bookmarks	Search for text in any of the bookmarks included.
Include Comment	Search for text in any of the comments.
Include Attachments	Search for text in any attached file of the PDF document.
Proximity	Search for multiple words or words in a document. A document is considered a match only if the search words are separated by not more than 900 words. This check box is available only when you select the **Match All of the words** option from the **Return results containing** drop-down list.
Stemming	Search for a single word and find the word as well as occurrences of the word ending in -ing, -ed, -s, and much more.

 Wildcard characters (*, ?) cannot be used while performing a search using the **Stemming** option.

Boolean Operators

Commonly used Boolean operators include "And" (used between two words to find documents that contain both terms), "Not" (used before a search term to exclude any documents that contain that term), "Or" (used to search for all instances of either term), "^" (used to search for all instances that have either term but not both, and "( )" (used to specify the order of evaluation of terms).

Bates Numbering

Bates numbering is a method used to sequentially number multiple documents for easy identification and retrieval. You can include a prefix and a suffix to a Bates number, and it can be either numeric or alphanumeric. Bates numbers appear in the header or footer of PDF documents.

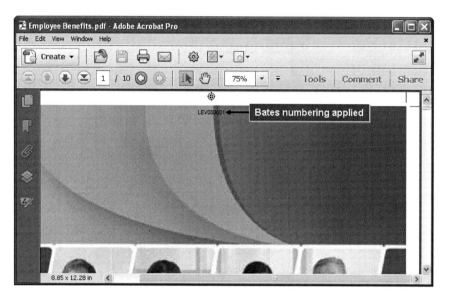

Figure 5-3: Bates Numbering applied to a PDF document.

Choosing Files for Bates Numbering

The files you choose for Bates numbering must not contain forms, encryption, digital signature fields, and security settings. If any one of these features is present in the chosen file, Adobe Acrobat will reject the file and display the message: "The following files cannot be used for Bates Numbering." The remaining content of the message will show the file name and state the reason for rejecting the file. When designating documents for Bates numbering, you can add PDFs and non-PDF files that can be converted to PDF.

How to Search Multiple PDF Documents

Procedure Reference: Add Metadata

To add metadata:

1. Choose **File→Properties.**

2. In the **Document Properties** dialog box, select the **Description** tab and in the **Description** section, click in the desired text box and specify the required details.

3. Click **OK** to close the dialog box.

Procedure Reference: Search Multiple PDF Documents

To search multiple PDF documents:

1. If necessary, display the Search window.

2. If necessary, click **New Search.**

3. In the **What word or phrase would you like to search for** text box, type the word or phrase you want to search for.

4. In the **Where would you like to search** section, select the **All PDF Documents in** option.

5. From the **All PDF Documents in** drop-down list, select **Browse for Location.**

6. In the **Browse For Folder** dialog box, navigate to and select the folder whose contents you want to search and click **OK.**

7. In the Search window, specify the search options.

8. Click **Search.**

9. If necessary, from the **Sort by** drop-down list, select the required sorting option.

10. If necessary, navigate to each occurrence of the search word.

Procedure Reference: Specify Advanced Search Options

To specify advanced search options:

1. If necessary, display the Search window.

2. If necessary, click **New Search.**

3. If necessary, in the **What word or phrase would you like to search for** text box, type the desired search term.

4. Click the **Show More Options** link.

5. From the **Look In** drop-down list, select the desired option.

    ● Specify the options to perform an index-based search.

        a. Select **Select Index.**

        b. In the **Index selection** dialog box, select the index you want to search and click **OK.**

    ● Select the desired location to perform the search in.

6. From the **Look In** drop-down list, select an appropriate folder.

7. If necessary, from the **Return results containing** drop-down list, select an option to refine your search.

8. If necessary, in the **Use these additional criteria** section, specify the desired options.

9. Click **Search.**

10. If necessary, navigate to each occurrence of the search word.

11. Close the Search window.

 An index must be created for an index search to be performed.

Procedure Reference: Add Bates Numbering

To add Bates numbering:

1. Choose **View→Tools→Pages.**

2. In the **Pages** section, in the **Edit Page Design** section, select the **Bates Numbering** option to display the drop-down list.

3. From the **Bates Numbering** drop-down list, select **Add Bates Numbering.**

4. In the Bates Numbering window, click **Add Files** and from the drop-down list, select the desired option.
   - Select **Add Files** and in the **Add Files** dialog box, select the desired files to which you want to add the Bates number and click **OK.**
   - Select **Add Folders** and in the **Browse For Folder** dialog box, select the desired folder to which you want to add the Bates number and click **OK.**
   - Select **Add Open Files** and in the **Open PDF Files** dialog box, click **Add Files** to add the Bates number for opened files and click **OK.**

5. If necessary, rearrange the files in the order in which you want the Bates number to appear.
   - Click and drag the file up or down or;
   - Select the file and click **Move Up** or **Move Down.**

6. If necessary, select any of the files and click **Remove** to remove them from the list.

7. Click **OK.**

8. In the **Add Header and Footer** dialog box, click in the appropriate header or footer text box and click **Insert Bates Number.**

9. In the **Bates Numbering Options** dialog box, specify the required settings.
   - In the **Number of Digits** text box, type a number between 3 and 15 to specify how many digits you want to assign to the Bates number.
   - In the **Start Number** text box, type a number you would like to assign to the first PDF on the list.
   - In the **Prefix** and **Suffix** text boxes, type any text that you want to display before and after the Bates number.

10. Click **OK** to apply the **Bates Numbering Options** settings.

11. In the **Add Header and Footer** dialog box, click **OK.**

12. Click **OK** to close the **Adobe Acrobat** message box.

13. If necessary, display and verify the page numbers for documents to which you applied the Bates numbering.

14. If necessary, choose **Tools→Pages→Bates Numbering→Remove** to remove the Bates numbering applied to a file.

ACTIVITY 5-2
Searching Multiple PDF Documents

Data Files:

C:\084548Data\Working with Multiple PDF Documents\Employee Benefits.pdf,
C:\084548Data\Working with Multiple PDF Documents\2010-2011 Benefits Change.pdf

Scenario:

While reviewing the Employee Benefits guide, you want to look for information on policies that would be beneficial to your coworkers.. You decide to search for the beneficial policy in the Employee Benefits guide. Also, you would like to assign a unique identifier to updated policies in the Employee Benefits guide for easy identification and future reference.

---

1. Search for instances of the word "policy."

    a. From the C:\084548Data\Working with Multiple PDF Documents folder, open the Employee Benefits.pdf file.

    b. Choose **Edit→Advanced Search.**

    c. In the **Where would you like to search** section, select the **All PDF Documents in** option.

    d. From the **All PDF Documents in** drop-down list, select **Browse for Location.**

    e. In the **Browse For Folder** dialog box, navigate to the C:\084548Data\Working with Multiple PDF Documents folder and click **OK.**

    f. In the **What word or phrase would you like to search for** text box, double-click and type *policy*

    g. In the Search window, check the **Whole words only** check box and click **Search.**

---

2. View the occurrences of the word "policy."

    a. In the **Results** list box, expand the second search result.

    b. In the expanded list, click the second occurrence of the word "policy."

    c. Observe the word "policy" is highlighted in the document pane.

---

3. Locate all documents containing any of the words in the search text.

    a. In the Search window, click **New Search.**

    b. At the bottom of the Search window, click the **Show More Options** link.

    c. From the **Return results containing** drop-down list, select **Match Any of the words.**

    d. From the **Look In** drop-down list, select **C:\084548Data\Working with Multiple PDF Documents.**

    e. In the Search window, click **Search.**

---

      f.   In the **Results** list box, expand the first search result.

      g.   In the expanded list, click the first occurrence of the word "policy" to view it in the 2010–2011 Benefits Change.pdf document.

4.   Search for the word "plans" in the documents.

      a.   In the Search window, click **New Search.**

      b.   In the **What word or phrase would you like to search for** text box, type *plans*

      c.   In the **Use these additional criteria** section, in the first set of connected options, from the first drop-down list, select **Subject** and click **Search.**

      d.   In the **Results** list box, expand the first search result.

      e.   From the expanded list, click the word "plans" to view the search result.

      f.   Close the Search window.

5.   Select the 2010–2011 Benefits Change.pdf document to assign a Bates number.

      a.   Choose **View→Tools→Pages.**

      b.   In the **Pages** section, in the **Edit Page Design** section, from the **Bates Numbering** drop-down menu, choose **Add Bates Numbering.**

      c.   In the Bates Numbering window, from the **Add Files** drop-down menu, choose **Add Open Files.**

      d.   In the **Open PDF Files** dialog box, hold down **Shift** and select the **Employee Benefits.pdf** file.

      e.   Click **Add Files.**

      f.   Observe that the Employee Benefits.pdf and 2010–2011 Benefits Change.pdf files are added to the list.

      g.   In the Bates Numbering window, click **OK.**

6.   Add Bates numbering to the selected documents.

      a.   In the **Add Header and Footer** dialog box, click in the **Center Footer Text** text box and click **Insert Bates Number.**

      b.   In the **Bates Numbering Options** dialog box, click in the **Prefix** text box, type *LEV* and then click **OK.**

      c.   In the **Add Header and Footer** dialog box, click **OK.**

      d.   In the **Adobe Acrobat** message box, click **OK.**

      e.   Switch to the Employee Benefits.pdf document.

      f.   Save the file as *Employee Benefits_Bates* in the PDF format.

      g.   Switch to the 2010–2011 Benefits Change.pdf document.

      h.   Save the file as *2010–2011 Benefits Change_Bates* in the PDF format.

7.   View the Bates numbering across both the documents.

a. Scroll down to view the footer section of the page.

b. Observe that the Bates number "LEV000002" appears on the page displayed in the document pane.

c. Scroll down to the end of the last page.

d. Observe that the Bates number "LEV00004" appears as a footer on the last page in the document.

e. Close the **2010–2011 Benefits Change_Bates.pdf** file.

f. Navigate to page i.

g. Scroll down to view the Bates number in the footer section.

h. Observe that the Bates number in this file starts from "LEV00005", appearing sequentially and continuing from the Employee Benefits.pdf document.

i. Close the Employee Benefits.pdf file.

Lesson 5 Follow-up

In this lesson, you worked with various documents. By securing the content, you will be able to control the access of PDF documents and by using the search options available in Acrobat, you will be able to quickly locate related information and work on them simultaneously.

1. **What is the best way to secure a PDF document?**

2. **How will controlling access to PDF documents help you in your job?**

6 | Reviewing PDF Documents

Lesson Time: 45 minutes

Lesson Objectives:

In this lesson, you will review a PDF document.

You will:

- Initiate a review.

- Review a PDF document.

- Compare PDF documents.

Introduction

You created, grouped, and sent PDF documents to other users and also received documents from them. Now, you may need to facilitate user feedback or give feedback to users about their document content. In this lesson, you will initiate and participate in PDF document reviews.

You generated a PDF document and distributed it to other users. You receive user feedback that there are some misspelled words in the PDF document. These errors could have been removed if the document had been reviewed before distribution.

TOPIC A
Initiate a Review

You worked with multiple PDF documents. You may now want to invite reviewers to review your document. In this topic, you will initiate a review.

Before a document is sent for review, you need to perform certain tasks such as identifying the type of review that will be most effective. Initiating the right type of review will enable you to interact with reviewers and generate an error-free document.

Collaboration Workflows in Acrobat

Using Acrobat X Pro, you can set up a collaboration review, invite participants, and track the responses from reviewers. To initiate a review, you need a PDF document, an email application, and an email server connection. Based on the review type you choose, you can initiate a PDF document review workflow.

Review Type	Description
Shared review	A review in which the participants can read and respond to each other's comments whether they review the PDF document on a local machine, as an email attachment, or on a remote server. The comments are stored in a repository on Acrobat.com or on an internal server. Shared review contains more details about the active review. The Notification feature enables you to track the availability of newly added comments and information about all recent review activities every time the PDF is opened.
Email-based review	A review ideal for collecting feedback from individuals who do not have access to a remote server. The initiator sends a PDF to reviewers as an email attachment. The reviewers review the document, add their comments, and send the document back to the initiator by replying to the comments. The initiator can then merge these comments into the master copy.
Collaborate Live review	A review that lets participants open and share PDF documents in a live chat session. In such sessions, the participants view a document within a live chat window.
Manual review	A review in which the initiator manually incorporates comments from each reviewer into the original PDF document. In this type of workflow, the reviewed document may be distributed through email, but the email application does not communicate directly with Acrobat.

The Review Tracker

The Tracker window contains information about documents sent for review. The window is split into two panes. The details of the option selected in the left pane are displayed in the right pane. This information includes reviews that have been updated, reviews sent, reviews received, servers to which the reviewed documents are sent, and details on the comments. It also includes information about the number of forms distributed and received. You can create a shared review or an email-based review, and create and distribute forms using the links in the right pane of the Tracker window.

Online Services

You can easily upload large documents and store them in the online workspace at Acrobat.com. Also, you can use the online services at Acrobat.com to easily share and send them to individuals within or outside an organization.

Tracking Forms

PDF forms that allow you to collect data from users can be tracked after they are distributed. After the user receives the form, they will fill in the fields and submit the data. The review tracker helps you to track the data input in the forms.

How to Initiate a Review

Procedure Reference: Initiate a Shared Review

To initiate a shared review:

1. Open the PDF file that needs to be sent for review.
2. If necessary, choose **Edit→Preferences** and in the **Categories** pane, select the **Reviewing** category and specify the shared review preferences.
3. In the **Comment** panel, in the **Review** section, click **Send for Shared Review.**
4. In the **Send for Shared Review** wizard, from the **How do you want to collect comments from your reviewers** drop-down list, select the desired option.
   - Select **Automatically download & track comments with Acrobat.com** to enable the reviewers to access the document from the Acrobat.com website.
   - Select **Automatically collect comments on my own internal server** to store the document in the shared folder and send it as a link to the reviewers.
5. If necessary, check the **Remember my choice** check box.
6. Click **Next.**
7. Specify the details for the default review message to be sent to the reviewers.
   - Specify information for the **Automatically download & track comments with Acrobat.com** review mode.
     a. In the **Send for Shared Review** dialog box, in the **Adobe ID (email address)** text box, type your Adobe ID.
     b. In the **Password** text box, type your password.
     c. Click **Sign In.**
   - Specify information for the **Automatically collect comments on my own internal server** review mode.
     a. In the **Send for Shared Review** dialog box, in the **Where would you like to internally host your shared review file** section, select the folder where you would like to save your document.

    b.   In the **Type the path to the shared network folder** section, in the text box, type the path or URL of the folder or browse to the desired folder and click **Next.**

    c.   In the **How do you want to distribute your shared review file** section, select the desired option.

    d.   In the **How do you want the shared review file to appear when it is sent** section, select the desired option and click **Next.**

    e.   In the **Provide a name for this server profile** text box, type a name for the server profile you use and click **Next.**

8.   In the **Send for Shared Review** dialog box, fill in the required details and click **OK.**

9.   The email message to be sent to the reviewer is displayed. In the **To** text box, type the email address of the person to whom you want to send the document, or choose contacts from your address book.

10.   If necessary, in the **CC** text box, type the email address of people to whom you want to send a copy of the document.

11.   If necessary, click the **Reset default message** link and customize the message.

12.   If necessary, click the **Review Deadline** link, and in the **Change Review Deadline** dialog box, specify a deadline for the reviewers to review the document and click **OK.**

13.   Click **Send** to send the message to the reviewers.

14.   In the **Outgoing Message Notification** message box, click **OK** to confirm the sending of the message.

Procedure Reference: Initiate an Email-Based Review

To initiate an email-based review:

1.   In the **Comment** panel, in the **Review** section, click **Send for Email Review** to display the **Getting Started** dialog box.

2.   Enter your identity information in the **Identity Setup** dialog box and click **Complete** to display the **Getting Started** wizard.

3.   On the **Getting Started** page, in the **Getting Started: Initiating an Email-Based Review** section, click **Browse** to display the **Open** dialog box.

4.   Navigate to the desired location and select the file you want to send for review.

5.   Click **Open** and then click **Next.**

6.   On the **Invite Reviewers** page, type the email address of the reviewer and click **Next.**

7.   On the **Preview Invitation** page, view the default email message displayed for your reviewer.

8.   Click **Send Invitation** to send the message.

9.   In the **Outgoing Message Notification** dialog box, click **OK** to send the file to your reviewer for review.

Procedure Reference: Collaborate Live on Acrobat.com

To send and collaborate live on Acrobat.com:

1.   Open the desired PDF document.

2.   In the **Comment** panel, in the **Review** section, click **Collaborate Live.**

3.   In the **Send and Collaborate Live** dialog box, click **Next.**

4.   Sign in to Acrobat.com with your Adobe user ID (email address) and password.

5. In the **Send and Collaborate Live** dialog box, in the **To** text box, type the desired email address.

6. If necessary, click the **Reset default message** link and customize the email message.

7. If necessary, check the **Store file on Acrobat.com and send a link to recipients** check box.

8. Click **Send.**

Procedure Reference: Track Reviews in a PDF Document

To track the review comments in a PDF document:

1. Display the Tracker window.

   ● In the **Comment** panel, in the **Review** section, click **Track Reviews** or;

   ● Choose **View→Comment→Review→Track Reviews.**

2. If necessary, in the left pane, click the **Sent** link to view the link to the documents you have sent for review.

3. Click the link to the document whose details you want to view.

4. In the **View Comments** section, click the **View Comments** link to view the comments given by the reviewers of the document.

5. If necessary, click the **Change Deadline** link to change the deadline for the review.

6. If necessary, specify the desired option in the **Reviewers** section.

   ● Click the **Email All Reviewers** link to send an email to all the reviewers.

   ● Click the **Add Reviewers** link to send the document to more reviewers.

   ● Click the **Start New Review with Same Reviewers** link to send another file for review.

7. If necessary, in the **View Comments** section, click the **End Review** link to end the review.

8. If necessary, in the left pane of the Tracker window, click the **Joined** link to view the PDF documents that have come for your review.

Procedure Reference: Upload Files to Acrobat.com

To upload files to Acrobat.com:

1. In the **Share** panel, in the **Send Files** section, click **Use Adobe SendNow Online.**

2. If necessary, sign in to Acrobat.com using your Adobe ID and password or sign up for a new ID.

3. In the **Select Any Type of File** section, click the **Add File** link to display the **Select File** dialog box.

 If the document is open, Acrobat by default adds it for uploading.

4. Select the file that you want to upload and click **Add.**

5. If necessary, in the **Select Any Type of File** section, click **Delete** to remove the selected file.

6. Click the **To** link and include the recipients' email addresses.

7. In the **Subject** and **Message** text boxes, include the appropriate information.

8. Click **Send Link** to upload the document.

A message stating that the document upload is completed and that the recipients have been emailed a link to the file on SendNow.Adobe.com will be displayed in the **Share** panel.

9. Click the **View and Track Sent File** link to view the document.
10. In the Acrobat.com website, in the **Share** dialog box, sign in with your Adobe ID and password.

The document will be displayed as a thumbnail in the lower pane of the browser window.

ACTIVITY 6-1
Initiating a Shared Review on a Network Folder

Data Files:

C:\084548Data\Reviewing PDF Documents\Employee Benefits.pdf

Scenario:

You created a draft HR policy document for your company. You compiled the information from various sources in a single PDF document. You want to send it to the senior management for a review.

---

1. Specify that the file's comments can use an author identity other than the computer login name.

    a. From the C:\084548Data\Reviewing PDF Documents folder, open the Employee Benefits.pdf document.

    b. Choose **Edit→Preferences.**

    c. In the **Preferences** dialog box, in the **Categories** list box, select **Commenting** to display the commenting preferences.

    d. In the **Making Comments** section, uncheck the **Always use Log-in Name for Author name** check box and then click **OK** to use an author identity different from the computer login name.

---

2. Initiate the shared review.

    a. Select the **Comment** panel and expand the **Review** section.

    b. In the **Review** section, click **Send for Shared Review.**

    c. In the **Send for Shared Review** wizard, from the **How do you want to collect comments from your reviewers** drop-down list, select **Automatically collect comments on my own internal server** and click **Next.**

    d. In the **Where would you like to internally host your shared review file** section, verify that the **Network folder** option is selected.

    e. In the **Type the path to the shared network folder** text box, type *192.168.50.227*\ *Shared*\ and click **Next.**

    f. In the **How do you want to distribute your shared review file** section, verify that the **Send it automatically using Adobe Acrobat** option is selected.

    g. In the **How do you want the shared review file to appear when it is sent** section, select the **As a link within the message** option and click **Next.**

    h. In the **Provide a name for this server profile** text box, triple-click, type *Adobe Acrobat* and then click **Next.**

"This information identifies you to all reviewers" page of the **Send for Shared Review** wizard is displayed only for the first time and students will need to specify their name and email details.

3. Specify your identity details.

   a. In the **Send for Shared Review** wizard, in the **Email Address (required field)** text box, type your email address and then press **Tab.**

   b. In the **Name (required field)** text box, type your name.

   c. Click **Next** to display the review message to be sent to the reviewers of the document.

   d. If necessary, in the **Send for Shared Review** wizard, type the file name as *Employee Benefits_review_student#* and click **Continue.**

"#" denotes the student ID assigned for each student.

4. Send the review message to the reviewers.

   a. In the **Send for Shared Review** wizard, in the **To** text box, type your partner's email ID.

   b. Click the **Review Deadline** link.

   c. In the **Change Review Deadline** dialog box, select the **No deadline** option and click **OK.**

   d. Click **Send.**

   e. In the **Outgoing Message Notification** message box, click **OK.**

TOPIC B
Review a PDF Document

You have your document ready for review, and you have initiated the review process by inviting other reviewers. Now, you may receive documents for review. In this topic, you will mark up a PDF document.

There may be different kinds of changes that a reviewer might suggest after going through a document. Different tools are available for suggesting these changes. It is important to use the right tool for giving an appropriate feedback.

Stamps

Stamps are tools used to inform users of the sensitivity or of the status of a PDF document. Based on the requirement, you can select a stamp from a palette of built-in stamps from the **Comment** panel. Dynamic stamps and Standard Business stamps primarily indicate the status of the document. Signature stamps guide the reviewer in placing a signature. You can customize a stamp and change the orientation of a stamp by moving the mouse pointer over the center handle at the top of the stamp.

Figure 6-1: Stamp attested in a PDF document.

Comments

Definition:

Comments are review tools used by a reviewer. They allow the reviewer to give an opinion or a suggestion about specific content in a document. You can choose to show or hide comments in a document. Comments can be given in the form of pop-up notes, call-out text boxes, or plain text.

Example:

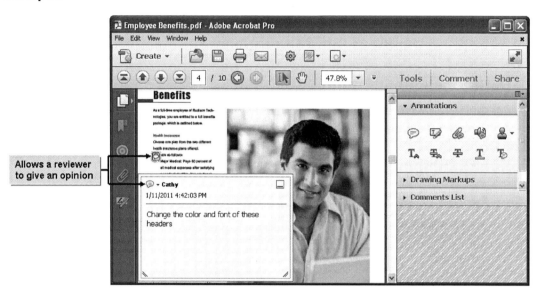

Figure 6-2: Options that aid in reviewing.

The Comment Panel

The **Comment** panel comprises various tools with which reviewers can add comments and other markups to a PDF document. Using the options in the panel, reviewers can choose appropriate markup tools to insert suggested modifications.

Option	Used To
Annotations	Include sticky notes, highlight text, or attach a file. Such options help reviewers annotate the content in a PDF document.
Drawing Markups	Draw multiple shapes such as free form, polygon, or cloud to create effects.
Review	Send a PDF document for shared, email-based, and live reviews.
Comments List	Display all the comments in a PDF document. It has a toolbar with options to sort, filter, and update comments. It can also be used to set commenting preferences.

The Commenting Process

The commenting process is a method to include or reply to review comments in a PDF document in an integrated manner. Using the options in the **Comments List** section, you can review and reply to comments in a methodical and consolidated way. Also, comments can quickly be searched using the **Filter comments** drop-down menu.

Annotations

The **Annotations** section provides multiple options to include different types of comments in a PDF document.

Button	Used To
Add sticky note (Ctrl+6)	Add sticky notes to any page in a document and position them anywhere on the page. When you add a sticky note to a document, a pop-up note is displayed. You can type your comments in the note. You can also make changes to the appearance of the pop-up note using the note properties.
Highlight text	Highlight text in different colors. You can also use them with notes.
Attach File	Attach a file at a specific location in a document.
Record Audio	Add an already recorded WAV or AIFF file as a comment or to record and place an audio comment in a document. Audio attachments appear in the Comments list and can be played back.
Insert text at cursor (Ins)	Type and insert text at the cursor position.
Replace (Ins)	Replace existing text matter with different information. You can include the text in the pop-up note that opens when the button is clicked.
Strikethrough (Del)	Delete the desired text. When the text is deleted, a strikethrough line appears. You can customize the color of the line.
Underline	Select the text and include an underline, or click the button and double-click the text that needs to be underlined.
Add stamp	Include stamp in a PDF document.
Add note to text	Include notes in a PDF document.

Drawing Markups

The **Drawing Markups** section has various shapes using which comments can be included while reviewing a PDF document.

Button	Used To
Add text box	Create a box that contains text in a PDF document. You can position it anywhere on the page and adjust it to any size.
Add text callout	Create text box markups that point to specific areas in a PDF document.
Draw line; draw straight line by holding Shift key	Draw lines across the area where you want the markup to appear.
Draw arrow; draw straight arrow by holding Shift key	Draw arrows across the area where you want the markup to appear.
Draw oval; draw circle by holding Shift key	Draw ovals in the area where you want the markup to appear.
Draw rectangle; draw square by holding Shift key	Draw rectangles across the area where you want the markup to appear.
Draw cloud; to complete cloud click the start point	Create closed shapes with multiple segments. The shapes contain curves, but not straight lines. You can also use them with notes.

Button	Used To
Draw polygon; to complete polygon click the start point	Create closed polygon shapes with multiple segments.
Draw connected lines; to end lines double-click last point	Create closed shapes in a connected manner.
Draw free form	Create free-form drawings. You can also use them with notes.
Erase free form by clicking and dragging	Erase free-form shapes and drawings.

How to Review a PDF Document

Procedure Reference: Participate in a Shared Review

To participate in a shared review:

1. In Microsoft Outlook, select the email you received.
2. Read the message and click the link given to open the document.
3. If necessary, in the **Adobe Acrobat Shared Review** message box, click **Connect.**
4. In the **Welcome Back to Shared Review** message box, click **OK** to begin your review.
5. Review the document using the review and markup tools in the **Comment** panel.
6. If necessary, on the document message bar, click **Publish Comments** to publish the review comments.
7. Save the document.

Procedure Reference: Participate in an Email-Based Review

To participate in an email-based review:

1. In Microsoft Outlook, select the email message you received.
2. Read the message and double-click the attached file to view it.
3. Review the file and add comments using the options in the **Comment** panel.
4. Save and close the document.
5. Send it back to the reviewer as an email attachment.

Procedure Reference: Specify the Author Name for Selected Comments

To specify the author name for selected comments:

1. In the PDF document, right-click any comment and choose **Properties.**
2. In the selected comment's **Text Box Properties** dialog box, select the **General** tab.
3. In the **Author** text box, type the author name you want to use and click **OK** to change the author name for the comment you selected.
4. If necessary, right-click the comment whose author name you changed and then choose **Make Current Properties Default** to set the custom author name for all new sticky note comments.

Procedure Reference: Attach a File as a Comment

To attach a file as a comment:

1. In Acrobat, open the document you want to review and in the **Comment** panel, in the **Annotations** section, click the **Attach File** button.
2. Click in the location in the document where you want to place the attachment.
3. In the **Add Attachment** dialog box, navigate to and select the file you want to attach and click **Open.**
4. In the **File Attachment Properties** dialog box, select the **Appearance** tab, specify the icon you want to display in the document to indicate the presence of the attachment, and specify the icon's color and opacity.
5. Select the **General** tab, specify the author, subject, and description for the attachment, and click **OK** to close the **File Attachment Properties** dialog box.
6. If required, save the document with a new name.

Procedure Reference: Add Stamps to PDF Documents

To add stamps to PDF documents:

1. In the **Comment** panel, in the **Annotations** section, from the **Stamp** drop-down menu, choose the desired stamp category and select the desired stamp.
2. In the document, click in a specific location where you want to add the stamp, or click and drag to specify the location and the size of the stamp.
3. If necessary, make the desired changes to the stamp's appearance.
   - Position the mouse pointer on the stamp, and click and drag to the desired position.
   - Select the stamp and drag any of the corner transform handles to resize the stamp.
   - Right-click the stamp, choose **Properties,** and specify the stamp's color or opacity on the **Appearance** tab.

Procedure Reference: Add Custom Stamps

To add custom stamps:

1. In the **Comment** panel, in the **Annotations** section, from the **Stamp** drop-down menu, choose **Custom Stamps.**
2. Select the **Create Custom Stamps** option to display the **Select Image for Custom Stamp** dialog box.
3. Click **Browse,** and in the **Open** dialog box, navigate to and select the file you want to use, and click **Open.**

4. If the file has more than one page, scroll to the page you desire and click **OK** to close the **Select Image for Custom Stamp** dialog box.

5. In the **Create Custom Stamp** dialog box, from the **Category** drop-down list, select the desired category or type a name in the **Category** text box to create a category.

6. In the **Name** text box, type a name for the custom stamp and click **OK.**

7. From the **Stamp** drop-down menu, choose the desired stamp category and from the selected stamp category's submenu, choose the custom stamp.

8. Click in the location in the document where you want to place the custom stamp.

9. Save the document.

Procedure Reference: Add Review Comments to a PDF Document

To add review comments to a PDF document:

1. In the **Comment** panel, in the **Annotations** section, select the review tool you want to use.

2. Click in the location where you want to add the comment and add the comment.

ACTIVITY 6-2
Reviewing PDF Documents

Data Files:

C:\084548Data\Reviewing PDF Documents\Employee Benefits review.pdf

Before You Begin:

Open the Microsoft Outlook application.

Scenario:

Your team has completed work on the Employee Benefits guide. You now need to have a look at it before releasing it to all the employees.

---

1. Open the file that has been sent to you for review.

    a. Observe that you have received a new email message from your partner with an invitation to the shared review.

    b. Select the email message.

    c. In the **Reading** pane, click the *<\\192.168.50.227\shared\Employee Benefits_ review.pdf>* link to open the PDF.

    d. In the **Adobe Acrobat Shared Review** message box, click **Connect.**

    e. In the **Welcome to Shared Review** message box, click **OK.**

---

2. Add review comments to the document.

    a. Navigate to page 1.

    b. In the left column, in the first paragraph, in the third line, click before the text "which is outlined below."

    c. In the **Comment** panel, in the **Annotations** section, click the **Insert text at cursor** button.

    d. In the pop-up window that is displayed, type *each of*

    e. Click the **minimize** icon to close the pop-up window.

    f. In the **Health Insurance** section, in the first line, double-click the word **"different."**

    g. In the **Comment** panel, in the **Annotations** section, click the **Strikethrough** button.

    h. Click the **Add sticky note** button.

    i. Click above the image on the right side of the "Benefits" page, and in the pop-up window, type *Try to change this image*

    j. Click the **minimize** icon to close the pop-up window.

    k. Close the **Comment** panel by selecting it again.

---

3. Publish the comments.

    a.   On the document message bar, click **Publish Comments.**

    b.   Choose **File→Save As→PDF.**

    c.   If necessary, in the **Save As** dialog box, navigate to the C:/084548Data/Reviewing PDF Documents folder.

    d.   In the **File** name text box, type ***Employee Benefits_review_student#*** and click **Save.**

    e.   Close the Employee Benefits_review_student#.pdf file.

    f.   Close the Microsoft Outlook application.

TOPIC C
Compare PDF Documents

You reviewed PDF documents. While reviewing a document, you may come across two copies that look the same, and you may not know which one is the final version. In this topic, you will compare PDF documents.

After the review, comparing the original version of a document with the reviewed version will help you identify the mistakes you made while authoring the document. This will help you avoid repeating mistakes in future projects.

The Compare Documents Feature

The Compare Documents feature can be used to find out the difference between two versions of a PDF document. You can choose two different versions of a document and specify the page range to be compared. The compared results not only display a summary but also highlight the differences between the documents.

How to Compare PDF Documents

Procedure Reference: Compare PDF Documents

To compare PDF documents:

1. In Acrobat X Pro, choose **View→Compare Documents** to display the **Compare Documents** dialog box.
2. Choose the first document for comparison.
   a. In the **Compare (older document)** section, click **Choose.**
   b. In the **Open** dialog box, select the file you want to open.
   c. Click **Open.**
   d. If necessary, in the **First page** and the **Last page** text boxes, specify the page numbers you want to include in the process of comparing the documents.
3. Choose the next document for comparison.
   a. In the **To (newer document)** section, click **Choose.**
   b. In the **Open** dialog box, select the file you want to open.
   c. Click **Open.**
   d. If necessary, in the **First page** and **Last page** text boxes, specify the page numbers you want to include in the process of comparing the documents.
4. In the **Document Description** section, select the description that is most appropriate for the documents you are comparing.
5. If necessary, check the **Compare text only** check box.
6. Click **OK.**
7. Navigate through the resultant document to view the differences between the compared documents.

Displaying the Compared Results

After you specify the required options in the **Compare Documents** dialog box and the documents are analyzed, the results are displayed in a new file with the **Compare** panel open. A summary of the compared results are displayed on the first page of the result document. The resultant document contains annotations that indicate the difference between the two documents. You can customize the appearance of these changes in the **Compare** panel. You can hide the results using the **Hide Results** option in the **Compare** panel. You can also select the desired options from the drop-down lists in the **Compare** panel to specify the color scheme, opacity, thumbnail size, and other layout option of the resultant document.

Archiving a PDF Document

In order to compare a document before and after review, the reviewed version of the document has to be archived. Saving an archive copy of the review document will bring it out of the review mode. You can save an archived copy by clicking **Server status: OK (click button for more options)**. All the comments logged in by the reviewer will get saved. However, any new comment added in the archived copy cannot be published.

Procedure Reference: Save an Archived Copy of a Reviewed PDF Document

To save an archived copy of a reviewed PDF document:

1. Open the reviewed document.
2. On the document message bar, click the **Server status: Ok** drop-down arrow and select **Save as Archive Copy.**
3. If necessary, in the **Save and Work Offline** dialog box, navigate to the desired location where you want to save the file.
4. If necessary, in the **File name** text box, type a new name for the file.
5. Click **Save** to save the file.
6. In the **Adobe Acrobat** message box, click **OK** to get the document out of the review mode.

ACTIVITY 6-3
Comparing PDF Documents

Data Files:

C:\084548Data\Reviewing PDF Documents\Employee Benefits_review.pdf, C:\084548Data\
Reviewing PDF Documents\Employee Benefits.pdf

Before You Begin:

The Employee Benefits_review.pdf file is open.

Scenario:

Now that your document is back from review, you want to identify the mistakes you had made so that you do not repeat them.

1. View the comments published in the document.

    a. In the document pane, observe that a message saying "3 new comments were received. Click here to accept" is displayed.

    b. Click the link to accept the comments published in the document.

    c. In the **Comments** panel, in the **Comments List (3)** section, observe the list of comments in the document.

2. Open reviewed documents in the Tracker window.

    a. In the **Comment** panel, scroll down, and in the **Review** section, click **Track Reviews.**

    b. In the Tracker window, in the left pane, under the **Sent** category, double-click the **Employee Benefits_review_student#.pdf** file.

    c. In the Tracker window, in the left pane, under the **Joined** category, double-click the **Employee Benefits_review.pdf** file.

    d. Close the Tracker window.

3. Save an archive copy of the reviewed PDF document.

    a. On the document message bar, from the **Server status: Ok** drop-down menu, choose **Save as Archive Copy.**

    b. If necessary, in the **Save and Work Offline** dialog box, navigate to the C:\
    084548Data\Reviewing PDF Documents folder.

    c. In the **Save and Work Offline** dialog box, in the **File name** text box, verify that the file name is *Employee Benefits_archive* and click **Save.**

    d. In the **Adobe Acrobat** message box, click **OK.**

    e. Save and close the Employee Benefits_review.pdf file.

4. Choose the documents you want to compare.

    a.   Choose **View→Compare Documents.**

    b.   In the **Compare Documents** dialog box, in the **Compare (older document)** section, click **Choose.**

    c.   If necessary, in the **Open** dialog box, navigate to the C:\084548Data\Reviewing PDF Documents folder.

    d.   Select the **Employee Benefits.pdf** file and click **Open.**

    e.   In the **First page** and **Last page** text boxes, verify that **1** and **8** are displayed, respectively.

    f.   In the **To (newer document)** section, click **Choose.**

    g.   If necessary, in the **Open** dialog box, navigate to the C:\084548Data\Reviewing PDF Documents folder.

    h.   Select the **Employee Benefits_archive.pdf** file and click **Open.**

    i.   In the **First page** and in the **Last page** text boxes, verify that **1** and **8** are displayed, respectively.

    j.   In the **Document Description** section, select the **Reports, spreadsheets, magazine layouts** option and click **OK.**

---

5. Compare the differences between the two documents.

    a.   Observe that the [Compare New] Employee Benefits_archive - Adobe Acrobat Pro window is displayed with the **Compare** panel open and the first page as the **Summary** page with the date and time of comparison.

    b.   Click the **Get started: first change is on page 3** link to view the first change between the two documents.

    c.   Observe that in the **Compare** panel, in the page 3 thumbnail, a purple colored arrow is displayed below the thumbnail indicating a change in the page between the two documents.

    d.   Choose **File→Save As→PDF.**

    e.   In the **Save As** dialog box, in the **File name** text box, type the name of the file as *[Compare New] Employee Benefits_archived* and click **Save.**

    f.   Close all the files.

Lesson 6 Follow-up

In this lesson, you initiated and participated in a document review workflow and compared two versions of a document. The workflow helps you to save time and resources because print copies are not required, and all files can be sent electronically. It also helps the review initiator to quickly identify and fix errors.

1. **Which type of document review workflow will work best for you? Why?**

2. **Why do you think commenting is necessary while reviewing documents?**

7 Validating PDF Documents

Lesson Time: 20 minutes

Lesson Objectives:

In this lesson, you will validate a PDF document.

You will:

- Sign a PDF document digitally.
- Verify a digital signature.

Introduction

You initiated and participated in a collaborative review. After finalizing a document, you may want to distribute it to other users. Before that, however, you may need to authenticate it. In this lesson, you will digitally sign a document.

While distributing a document, you may want to be certain that the recipient receives the finalized copy of the document verified by you. By digitally signing a document, you can ensure that the intended recipient receives the signed document.

TOPIC A
Sign a PDF Document Digitally

As PDF documents become more and more accessible, the need to check the authenticity of such documents arises. This includes the ability to verify that a document is from a particular person and that the document has not been tampered with since it was sent. In this topic, you will digitally sign a document.

When you distribute your work, you may want to be certain that the intended recipients receive the copy. By enforcing security options, you can ensure the same.

Digital Signatures

A *digital signature* is a collection of information that uniquely identifies an individual. You need to create a digital ID to add a digital signature to a document. The digital signature will be listed within the **Signatures** panel. The signature may display a graphic element, such as a scanned signature or logo, or a name and information describing the purpose of the signature.

Figure 7-1: *Digital signature with unique identity details.*

Digital IDs

A *digital ID* is a type of identification that allows you to create a digital signature. It contains a name, an email address, a serial number, and an expiration date. It uses two keys: a public key and a private key. The public key locks or encrypts data; the private key unlocks or decrypts that data. While PDF documents are signed, the private key is used to apply digital signatures. The certificate that is distributed contains the public key and other identification details that are needed to validate a signature, or verify an identity.

You can either create a self-signed digital ID or obtain a digital ID from a third-party provider. A self-signed digital ID is sufficient for most situations. In case of business transactions, however, you may need a digital ID from a trusted third-party provider called certificate authority to prove your identity. You need to choose a certificate authority trusted by well-known companies doing business on the Internet for your signature to be acceptable.

The Adobe LiveCycle Rights Management Server

Adobe LiveCycle Rights Management server is a server-based security system that helps secure PDF documents. The process of using this security system involves four stages.

Stage	Description
Configure the policy server	When the system administrator of the company configures the Adobe LiveCycle Rights Management server, he can manage accounts and define organizational policies.
Publish a document with a security policy	When authors create PDF, they can apply a policy stored on the Adobe LiveCycle Rights Management server. The policy server generates a licence and assigns a unique encryption key to the PDF. Acrobat embeds this licence in the PDF and uses the encryption key to encrypt it. Either the author or the administrator can use the licence for tracking and auditing the PDF.
View a policy-applied document	When users attempt to open the secured PDF, they have to specify their identity. If the users have rights to access the PDF, it is decrypted and opened.
Administer events and modify access	When the author or the administrator logs in using the Adobe LiveCycle Rights Management server account, they can track events and change access to policy-secured PDFs. Events include activities such as applying a policy to a document, or opening a policy-protected document. Administrators can view all PDF and system events, and modify settings and access permission to policy-secured PDFs.

Using the Adobe LiveCycle Rights Management Server

Using the Adobe LiveCycle Rights Management server, you can consistently apply policies to control access and use of documents. You can make policy changes without having to reissue documents after they are distributed by simply changing policies, such as revoking access to a previously distributed document, changing usage rights, or adding an expiration date on the server.

Security Envelopes

A *security envelope* is an encrypted envelope that is used to transfer files through email. The files are added as attachments to the envelope. When using a security envelope, you can choose to encrypt only the attachments. Encrypting the attachment ensures that it cannot be modified unless it is saved to a hard disk.

The Sign & Certify Section

The **Sign & Certify** section has various options to sign and secure the content in a document. You can sign a document using a digital signature or an ink signature. You can certify the document with visible or invisible signatures. Using the options in the section, you can validate signatures, clear all signatures, and authenticate documents.

 A document can be certified with a signature only if it does not contain any other signatures.

The Signatures Panel

The **Signatures** panel displays information about each signature in the current document and the history of the document since the first signature. Each signature has an icon identifying its verification status. Verification details are listed beneath each signature and can be viewed by expanding the signature. The **Signatures** panel also provides you with information about the time when the document was signed, indicates if the document has been modified since signing, and displays details of the signer.

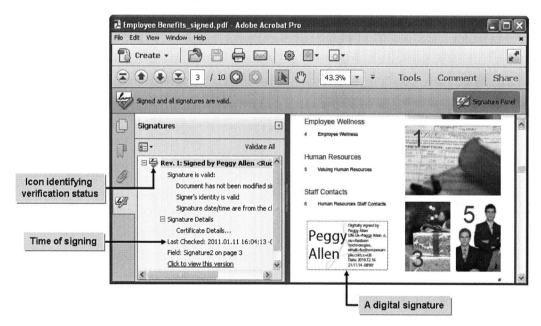

Figure 7-2: The Signatures Panel.

Signature Status Icons

When a document is digitally signed, a signature status icon identifying its current verification status is displayed on the document message bar.

Icon	Description
Blue Ribbon	This icon indicates that the certification is valid.
Digital Signature	This icon, along with the name of the signer in the **Signatures** panel, indicates the presence of a digital signature.

Icon	Description
Checkmark	This icon indicates that the signature is valid.
Red X	This icon indicates that the signature is invalid.
Question Mark	This icon indicates that the signature cannot be verified as the signer's certificate is not found in the list of trusted identities.
Caution Triangle	This icon indicates that the document has been modified after the signature was added.

The Signature Validation Status Dialog Box

The **Signature Validation Status** dialog box indicates the changes that have been made to a document after a signature is applied to it. If no changes have been made, it certifies that the document has not been modified since its certification.

Viewing Signature Fields

The **Signatures** button in the **Navigation Pane** can be used to display the **Signatures** panel. This panel lists the signatures in a PDF document. You can collapse a signature to see only the name, date, and status, or you can expand it to see more information.

 In situations where the signature is either unknown or not verified, you have to manually validate the signature to determine the cause of the problem and solve it. In case of an invalid signature, you have to contact the signer about the problem.

Validation Rules for Signature

When signatures are validated, an icon appears on the document message bar to indicate the signature status. Further details about the status appear in the **Signatures** panel and in the **Signatures Properties** dialog box. To ensure that signatures are validated when you open a PDF and that all verification details appear with the signature, you need to set your verification preferences in advance.

Protection Options

The **Protection** section has various options to secure a document. You can encrypt the document using a certificate or password so that only intended recipients can view the document. You can also embed the document in a security envelope and send the document as file attachments via email. The other tools are used to redact and remove specific content from a document.

Security Methods

Acrobat provides several methods of applying security to PDF documents.

Security Method	Used To
Digital signatures	Indicate approval of a PDF document or form that you filled out.
Password encryption	Add passwords and set security options in order to restrict the opening, editing, and printing of PDF documents.
Certification encryption	Encrypt a document so that only a specified set of users can access it.
Server-based security policies	Apply server-based security policies to PDF documents. This is especially useful if you want others to access PDF documents only for a limited time.
Custom security policy	Apply the same security settings to a number of PDF documents by creating a custom security policy.
Security envelopes	Send secure file attachments through email.

The Password Strength Meter

The password strength meter evaluates and indicates the password strength using various color options such as red, blue, dark green, and light green to rate as weak, medium, strong, and best for each password.

Security Policies

A security policy consists of a group of security settings that can be captured for reuse in multiple PDF documents.

Security Policy	Used To
Password security	Password protect documents.
Public key certificate security	Encrypt documents for a list of recipients. Creating policies for password and public key certificate security lets you reuse the same security settings for a set of documents without having to change them for each document.
Adobe LiveCycle Rights Management	Create and store policies on a server. Users must have access to the server to use them. You can use the Adobe LiveCycle Rights Management server if your company has purchased rights and made the server available to you.

AES 256 Algorithm for Password-Based Encryption

The Advanced Encryption Standard (AES) is the encryption standard used worldwide. The Adobe Acrobat 9 Pro application has an encryption level of 256-bit AES, which allows you to encrypt files to help maintain the confidentiality of proprietary information. You can encrypt all document contents, encrypt all document contents except metadata (Acrobat 6 and later compatible), or encrypt only file attachments (Acrobat 7 and later compatible).

Unicode Support for Passwords

You can encrypt your digital ID information by checking the **Enable Unicode Support** check box in the **Add Digital ID** wizard and by specifying the unicode values for the required fields. Unicode provides a unique number for every character, no matter what the program or language is.

How to Sign a PDF Document Digitally

Procedure Reference: Create a Digital ID

To create a digital ID:

1. Choose **File→Properties.**
2. In the **Document Properties** dialog box, select the **Security** tab.
3. In the **Document Security** section, from the **Security Method** drop-down list, select **Certificate Security.**
4. In the **Certificate Security Settings** wizard, specify the general settings and click **Next.**
5. In the **Document Security - Digital ID Selection** dialog box, in the **My Digital IDs** section, click **Add Digital ID.**
6. In the **Add Digital ID** wizard, select the desired options.

   - Select the **My existing digital ID from** option, click **Next,** and specify the desired options to create a digital ID from an existing digital ID.

     a. In the **File Name** text box, type the path of the file or click **Browse** and in the **Locate Digital ID File** dialog box, select the appropriate digital ID and click **Open.**

     b. In the **Password** text box, type the desired password and click **Next.**

     c. Click **Finish.**

   - Select the **A new digital ID I want to create now** option, click **Next,** and specify the desired options to create a self-signed digital ID.

     a. In the **Add Digital ID** wizard, select the desired option and click **Next.**

     b. In the **Name** text box, type your name.

     c. In the **Organizational Unit** text box, type the organization unit.

     d. In the **Organizational Name** text box, type the name of the organization.

     e. In the **Email Address** text box, type the email address and click **Next.**

     f. In the **Country/Region** drop-down list, select the country.

     g. If necessary, check the **Enable Unicode Support** check box to specify the desired unicode values.

     h. From the **Key Algorithm** and **Use digital ID for** drop-down lists, select the desired options.

     i. In the **Add Digital ID** wizard, in the **Password** text box, type the password and in the **Confirm Password** text box, retype the password.

     j. Click **Finish** to complete the process of creating a self-signed digital ID.

 The recent new digital ID information is displayed in the **My Digital IDs** section of the **Document Security - Digital ID Selection** dialog box.

7. Select the digital ID and click **OK.**

8. In **Certificate Security Settings** wizard, click **Next** and then click **Finish** to add the digital ID.

9. In the **Acrobat Security** message box, click **OK.**

10. In the **Document Properties** dialog box, click **OK.**

11. Save the document.

Procedure Reference: Digitally Sign a PDF Document

To digitally sign a PDF document:

1. In the **Tools** panel, in the **Sign & Certify** section, click **Sign Document** or **Place Signature.**

2. In the **Adobe Acrobat** message box, click **OK** to start signing the PDF.

3. Position the mouse pointer on the document page where you would like to place the signature, and click and drag to display the **Sign Document** dialog box.

4. From the **Sign As** drop-down list, select the ID you want to use.

5. In the **Password** text box, type a password.

6. If necessary, click **Info** to view the certificate details of the signature.

7. Click **Sign** to sign the document.

8. In the **Save As** dialog box, specify a new name for the document so that you can make any changes to the original PDF without invalidating the signature and click **Save.**

Procedure Reference: Export a Digital ID

To export a digital ID:

1. Choose **View→Tools→Protection.**

2. In the **Protection** section, from the **More Protection** drop-down menu, choose **Security Settings.**

3. In the **Security Settings** dialog box, in the left pane, select the digital ID that you want to export.

4. Click **Export** to export the digital ID.

5. In the **Data Exchange File - Export Options** wizard, in the **Export Options** section, perform the desired actions.

    ● Select the **Email the data to someone** option and then click **Next** to specify the desired options to share the digital ID through email.

        a. In the **Compose Email** dialog box, in the **Message** section, in the **To** text box, type an email address and click **Email.**

        b. In the **Microsoft Outlook** message box, click **OK.**

    ● Select the **Save the data to a file** option and then click **Next** to specify the desired options to save the digital ID in the desired location.

        a. In the **Export Data As** dialog box, click **Save** to save the certificate.

        b. In the **Acrobat Security** message box, click **OK.**

6. If necessary, click **Remove ID** to delete any ID from the list.

7. If necessary, click **Certificate Details** to view the details of your certificate and click **OK** to close it.

8. Close the **Security Settings** dialog box.

Procedure Reference: Share a Digital ID Certificate File

To share a digital ID certificate file:

1. Choose **View→Tools→Protection.**

2. In the **Protection** section, from the **More Protection** drop-down menu, choose **Security Settings.**

3. If necessary, click **Add ID** to create an ID or import an ID to the Windows certificate store.

4. In the **Security Settings** dialog box, from the list of IDs, select the ID you want to share.

5. If necessary, click **Remove ID** to delete any ID from the list.

6. If necessary, click **Certificate Details** to view the details of your certificate and click **OK** to close it.

7. In the **Security Settings** dialog box, click **Export.**

8. In the **Data Exchange File - Export Options** dialog box, select the desired option.

    *   Select the **Email the data to someone** option, click **Next,** and specify the desired options to share the digital ID through email.

        a.   In the **Compose Email** dialog box, type an email address.

        b.   Click **Email.**

    *   Select the **Save the data to a file** option, click **Next,** and specify the desired options to save the digital ID in the desired location.

        a.   In the **Export Data As** dialog box, click **Save** to save the certificate.

        b.   In the **Acrobat Security** message box, click **OK.**

9. Close the **Security Settings** dialog box.

Procedure Reference: Save a Document as a Certified Document

To save a document as a certified document:

1. Choose **File→Save as→Certified PDF.**

2. In the **Save as Certified Document** dialog box, click **OK.**

3. In the **Adobe Acrobat** dialog box, click **OK.**

4. Position the mouse pointer on the document page where you would like your digital signature to appear, and click and drag to display the **Certify Document** dialog box.

5. In the **Password** text box, type a password.

6. From the **Permitted Actions After Certifying** drop-down list, select the actions you want to allow for this document.

    *   Select **No changes allowed** to prevent any changes to the document.

    *   Select **Form fill-in and digital signatures** to allow form completion actions and to add digital signatures.

    *   Select **Annotations, form fill-in, and digital signatures** to allow commenting, form completion, as well as adding digital signatures.

7. Click **Sign.**

8. In the **Save As** dialog box, save the PDF using a different file name other than the original file and close the document without making additional changes.

Procedure Reference: Secure a Document Using a Security Envelope

To secure a document using a security envelope:

1. Choose **View→Tools→Protection.**
2. In the **Protection** section, from the **More Protection** drop-down menu, choose **Create Security Envelope.**
3. In the **Create Security Envelope** wizard, click **Add File to Send.**
4. In the **Files to Enclose** dialog box, navigate to and select the document to attach, and click **Open.**
5. If necessary, select any PDFs in the list that you do not want to include and click **Remove Selected Files.**
6. Click **Next.**
7. In the **Create Security Envelope** wizard, from the list of envelope templates, select the desired template and click **Next.**
8. Specify when you want to deliver the envelope and click **Next.**
9. Check the **Show all policies** check box and select a security policy, or click **New Policy** and create a policy.
10. Click **Next.**
11. Specify the appropriate identity information and click **Next.**
12. Click **Finish.**

ACTIVITY 7-1
Signing the Employee Benefits Guide Digitally

Data Files:

C:\084548Data\Validating PDF Documents\Employee Benefits.pdf

Scenario:

You want to forward the updated Employee Benefits Guide to all employees in your organization. But, you want to authenticate it so that users know that it is from you and that it was not changed after you had added your signature.

---

1. Create a digital ID.

   a. From the C:\084548Data\Validating PDF Documents folder, open the Employee Benefits.pdf file.

   b. Navigate to page iii.

   c. Choose **View→Tools→Sign & Certify**.

   d. In the **Sign & Certify** section, click **Sign Document**.

   e. In the **Adobe Acrobat** message box, click **OK**.

   f. On page iii, scroll down, draw a rectangle in the blank area below the "Staff Contacts" section to create a signature field.

   g. In the **Add Digital ID** wizard, in the **I want to sign this document using** section, select the **A new digital ID I want to create now** option and click **Next**.

   h. Verify that the **New PKCS#12 digital ID file** option is selected and click **Next**.

   i. In the **Name** text box, type *Peggy Allen* and press **Tab**.

   j. In the **Organizational Unit** text box, type *Rudison Technologies*

   k. In the **Email Address** text box, triple-click, type *peggy@ogc.com* and then click **Next**.

   l. In the **Password** text box, click, type *password* and then press **Tab**.

   m. In the **Confirm Password** text box, type *password* and click **Finish** to complete the process of creating a self-signed digital ID.

   n. Observe that the **Sign Document** dialog box is displayed with the digital ID in the middle of the dialog box.

   o. In the **Password** text box, click, type *password* and click **Sign**.

   p. In the **Save As** dialog box, in the **File Name** text box, type *Employee Benefits_signed* and click **Save**.

   q. Observe that the Peggy Allen digital ID, along with a green check mark below the toolbars is displayed, indicating that the Employee Benefits_signed.pdf document is signed.

2. Export the digital ID to send it to others.

    a.   Choose **View→Tools→Protection.**

    b.   In the **Protection** section, from the **More Protection** drop-down menu, choose **Security Settings.**

    c.   In the **Security Settings** dialog box, in the left pane, expand **Digital IDs** and **Digital ID Files.**

    d.   In the left pane, select the **PeggyAllen.pfx** digital ID and click **Export.**

    e.   In the **Data Exchange File - Export Options** dialog box, in the **Export Option** section, verify that the **Save the data to a file** option is selected and click **Next.**

    f.   In the **Export Data As** dialog box, navigate to the C:\084548Data\Validating PDF Documents folder.

    g.   Click **Save** to save the digital ID certificate.

    h.   In the **Acrobat Security** message box, click **OK** to close it.

    i.   Close the **Security Settings** dialog box.

    j.   Close the Employee Benefits_signed.pdf file.

3. Save the document as a certified PDF.

    a.   From the C:\084548Data\Validating PDF Documents folder, open the Employee Benefits.pdf file.

    b.   Choose **File→Save as→Certified PDF.**

    c.   In the **Save as Certified Document** dialog box, click **OK.**

    d.   In the **Adobe Acrobat** message box, click **OK.**

    e.   Navigate to page iii.

    f.   On page iii, scroll down, position the mouse pointer below the "Staff Contacts" sub-heading, and draw a rectangle to create the signature field.

    g.   In the **Certify Document** dialog box, in the **Sign As** drop-down list, verify that **Peggy Allen <peggy@ogc.com>** is selected.

    h.   Click in the **Password** text box and type *password*

    i.   In the **Permitted Actions After Certifying** drop-down list, verify that **Form fill-in and digital signatures** is selected and click **Sign.**

    j.   In the **Save As** dialog box, type *My Employee Benefits* and then click **Save.**

    k.   Observe that the Peggy Allen digital ID, along with a blue ribbon, is displayed below the toolbars, indicating that the My Employee Benefits.pdf document is certified.

    l.   Collapse the **Protection** section.

TOPIC B
Verify a Digital ID

You digitally signed a document. Sometimes, you may receive a digitally signed document, and you may want to check and make sure that the document is authentic. In this topic, you will verify digital signatures.

Acrobat provides you with tools necessary to verify digital signatures within a PDF. This allows you to make sure that the digital signature in the document you have received is authentic and that nobody has tampered with the document after it was signed by its original author.

How to Verify a Digital ID

Procedure Reference: Add a Digital ID Certificate from a File

To add a digital ID certificate from a file:

1. In the **Tools** panel, in the **Sign & Certify** section, from the **More Sign & Certify** drop-down menu, choose **Manage Trusted Identities.**
2. In the **Manage Trusted Identities** dialog box, click **Add Contacts.**
3. In the **Choose Contacts to Import** dialog box, click **Browse,** navigate to and select the digital ID certificate file, and click **Open.**
4. In the **Choose Contacts to Import** dialog box, in the **Contacts** section, select the desired contact.
5. In the **Certificates** section, select the displayed contact and in the **Certificate Viewer** dialog box, click **Details** to view the details of the certificate.
6. If necessary, contact the person from whom you received the file and verify that the given data is correct.
7. Click **OK** to close the **Certificate Viewer** dialog box.
8. If necessary, click **Trust** and in the **Import Contact Settings** dialog box, in the **Trust** section, specify the trust options and click **OK.**
9. In the **Choose Contacts to Import** dialog box, click **Import.**
10. In the **Import Complete** dialog box, click **OK.**
11. In the **Manage Trusted Identities** dialog box, click **Close** to close it.

Procedure Reference: Add a Digital ID Certificate from Email

To add digital ID certificates from email:

1. Open the digital certificate attachment in Acrobat.
2. In the **Data Exchange File - Import Contact** dialog box, click **Set Contact Trust.**
3. In the **Import Contact Settings** dialog box, click **Certificate Details** to view the details of the certificate in the **Certificate Viewer** dialog box.
4. If necessary, contact the person who sent the certificate and verify that the given data is correct.
5. Click **OK** to close the **Certificate Viewer** dialog box.
6. In the **Import Contact Settings** dialog box, click **OK** to close it.

7. In the **Import Complete** dialog box stating that the certificate is successfully imported, click **OK** to close it.

8. In the **Data Exchange File - Import Contact** dialog box, click **Close** to close it.

Procedure Reference: Obtain Digital ID Certificates from Signed Documents

To obtain digital ID certificates from signed documents:

1. Open the signed PDF document.

2. Display the **Signature Validation Status** dialog box.

   - Display the **Signatures** panel, select the digital signature, click the **Options** button, and choose **Validate Signature** or;

   - Click the digital signature on the document page.

3. Click **Signature Properties.**

4. In the **Signature Properties** dialog box, click **Show Certificate.**

5. In the **Certificate Viewer** dialog box, select the **Trust** tab and click **Add to Trusted Identities.**

6. In the **Acrobat Security warning** dialog box stating that you may need to re-validate any signatures if you change the trust settings, click **OK.**

7. If necessary, in the **Import Contact Settings** dialog box, in the **Trust** section, specify the trust settings and click **OK.**

8. In the **Certificate Viewer** dialog box, click **OK** to close it.

9. In the **Signature Properties** dialog box, click **Close** to close it.

Procedure Reference: Verify a Digital Signature

To verify a digital signature:

1. Open the PDF document containing the signature.

2. Display the **Signatures** panel.

3. Verify that the digital signature is authentic.

   - In the **Signatures** panel, select the digital signature, click the **Options** button, and choose **Validate Signature** or;

   - Click the digital signature on the document page.

 The **Signature Validation Status** dialog box is displayed, listing the verification status of the digital signature.

4. If the status is unknown, click **Signature Properties,** select the **Signer** tab, view the validity details of the signature, click **Show Certificate** to view the details of the certificate, and click **OK.**

5. In the **Signature Properties** dialog box, click **Close** to close it.

ACTIVITY 7-2
Verifying a Digital Signature

Data Files:

C:\084548Data\Validating PDF Documents\My Employee Benefits.pdf

Before You Begin:
The My Employee Benefits.pdf file is open.

Scenario:
You have signed the project report before distributing it to all employees in your organization. You have sent it for review to the head of the marketing department. The department head wants to authenticate the document.

---

1. Add Peggy Allen's digital ID certificate to your list of trusted identities.

   a. Click the digital signature of Peggy Allen on the document page.

   b. In the **Signature Validation Status** dialog box, click **Signature Properties.**

   c. In the **Signature Properties** dialog box, click **Show Certificate.**

   d. In the **Certificate Viewer** dialog box, select the **Trust** tab and click **Add to Trusted Identities.**

   e. In the **Acrobat Security** message box stating that you will need to re-validate any signatures if you change the trust settings, click **OK.**

   f. In the **Import Contact Settings** dialog box, on the **Trust** tab, verify that the **Use this certificate as a trusted root** and **Certified documents** check boxes are checked and click **OK.**

   g. In the **Certificate Viewer** dialog box, click **OK.**

   h. In the **Signature Properties** dialog box, click **Close.**

---

2. Verify whether the digital signature in the document is valid.

   a. On the document page, click Peggy Allen's digital signature.

   b. Observe that the **Signature Validation Status** dialog box is displayed indicating that the signature is valid. Click **Close.**

   c. Close the My Employee Benefits.pdf file.

Lesson 7 Follow-up

In this lesson, you validated a PDF document. This will help you to ensure the authenticity of the document.

1. **To what types of documents will you add a signature?**

2. **How will you secure a PDF document and which option will you prefer to use?**

8 | Converting PDF Files

Lesson Time: 20 minutes

Lesson Objectives:

In this lesson, you will optimize and convert PDF documents to other formats.

You will:

- Optimize PDF files.
- Convert PDF files to other formats.

Introduction

You validated PDF documents. You may now need to reduce the size of the PDF documents and convert them to other formats which will enable sharing of information. In this lesson, you will optimize and convert PDF documents.

Often, you may need to upload or send large files on the web or through email. Because there could be size limitations for uploading files or sending through email, you may not be able to quickly send critical documents. Acrobat provides you with options to reduce the file size for facilitating faster uploads.

TOPIC A
Optimize PDF Files

You validated PDF documents. You may now want to electronically distribute the document, keeping the file size as small as possible. In this topic, you will optimize a PDF document.

Users are prone to cancel the downloading of files that are too large because it may take so much time. Reducing the file size of PDF documents you generate helps you to quickly transfer them via email or upload them on the web.

Optimization

Definition:

Optimization of a PDF document is the process of reducing the file size of the document by removing embedded fonts, compressing images, and discarding objects and data that are no longer needed. Depending on the properties and the use of the file, you can determine how optimization needs to be done. You can also save the PDF as a reduced size PDF to compress a file.

Example:

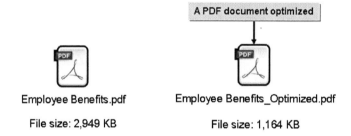

Employee Benefits.pdf

File size: 2,949 KB

Employee Benefits_Optimized.pdf

File size: 1,164 KB

Figure 8-1: An optimized PDF document.

The PDF Optimizer Dialog Box

The **PDF Optimizer** dialog box contains settings that help minimize the file size of a PDF document for easy access by compressing the file and its constituent parts. This dialog box allows you to change settings for PDF compatibility and to audit a document's space usage. You can compress a PDF file by setting a variety of properties such as those related to the image, font, and transparency. You can also remove metadata, file attachments, and other document information from the PDF file.

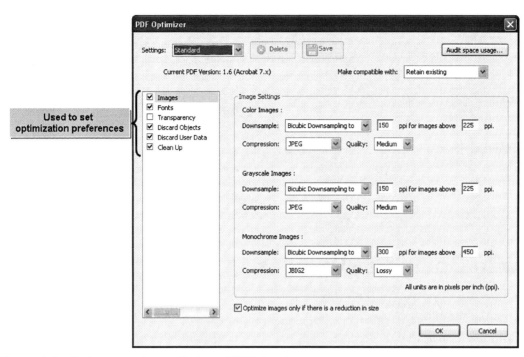

Figure 8-2: Options used to optimize a PDF document.

PDF Optimizer Options

The **PDF Optimizer** dialog box has a group of check boxes in the left pane for defining the optimizer settings to reduce a PDF file size.

Option	Description
Settings	A section that helps you to reduce the size of an image and make it compatible with Acrobat 7.0 or later versions. You can also customize the settings using the options.
Images	An option that helps you to set options for color, grayscale, and monochrome image compression.
Fonts	An option that helps you to embed and unembed fonts. If you know that the fonts used in your PDF document are already installed on the computers of the users who will use it, you can unembed those fonts. If you unembed a font that is not available to someone reading your PDF document, Acrobat will display a substitute font when the document is opened on their computer.
Transparency	An option that helps you to set transparency and flattener settings.
Discard Objects	An option that helps you to specify objects that you want to remove from the PDF document and convert smooth lines to curves, thereby reducing the size of PDF documents.
Discard User Data	An option that helps you to remove any hidden or confidential information such as metadata, file attachments, and links, that you do not want to share with other users.

Option	Description
Clean Up	An option that helps you to select an object conversion option and remove elements from the PDF document that you do not need.
Audit space usage	A button that helps you to identify the space occupied by the components of a PDF document such as fonts, images, graphics, and other information.
Make compatible with	A drop-down list that helps you to make a compressed version of a PDF document compatible with earlier or newer versions of Acrobat. You can also retain the existing version of Acrobat.

How to Optimize PDF Files

Procedure Reference: Reduce the File Size

To reduce the file size:

1. Open the desired PDF document.
2. Choose **File→Save As→Reduced Size PDF.**
3. In the **Reduce File Size** dialog box, from the **Make compatible with** drop-down list, select a newer version of Acrobat to obtain greater file size reduction.
4. If necessary, click **Apply to Multiple** to display the Arrange documents window to apply the compression settings to multiple files.
5. If necessary, in the Arrange documents window, from the **Add Files** drop-down menu, choose **Add Files** to include more files for compression.
6. In the Arrange documents window, click **OK.**
7. If necessary, in the **Output Options** dialog box, in the **Target Folder** section, choose the desired folder.
8. If necessary, in the **Output Options** dialog box, in the **File Naming** section, select the desired option.
9. If necessary, in the **Output Options** dialog box, check the **Overwrite existing files** check box to overwrite the existing document.
10. In the **Save As** dialog box, in the **File name** text box, type a new file name.
11. Click **Save.**

Procedure Reference: Optimize a PDF File

To optimize a PDF file:

1. Open the desired PDF document.
2. Choose **File→Save As→Optimized PDF** to open the **PDF Optimizer** dialog box.
3. If necessary, in the **PDF Optimizer** dialog box, from the **Make compatible with** drop-down list, select an option to make it compatible and, therefore, readable with older versions of Acrobat.

4.   If necessary, view the size of total files and elements.

    a.   Click **Audit space usage.**

    b.   In the **Audit space usage** message box, view the total size of files and elements and click **OK.**

5.   If necessary, in the **PDF Optimizer** dialog box, in the left pane, check the check box next to a panel option, and in the right pane, change the settings to compress the file size.

6.   Click **OK.**

7.   Save the optimized document as a new file or overwrite an existing document.

ACTIVITY 8-1
Optimizing a PDF Document

Data Files:

C:\084548Data\Converting PDF Files\Employee Benefits.pdf

Scenario:

You want to check the file size of the Employee Benefits.pdf file. Because you want to distribute it through email and the web, you want to keep the file size and resolution to a minimum and reduce the potential download time. You also need to ensure that the document is devoid of unnecessary and private information before being sent.

---

1. Optimize the Employee Benefits.pdf file by limiting the color and grayscale resolution to **100 ppi.**

    a. From the C:\084548Data\Converting PDF Files folder, open the Employee Benefits.pdf file.

    b. Choose **File→Save As→Optimized PDF.**

    c. In the **PDF Optimizer** dialog box, click **Audit space usage** to view the size of the components and other elements in the document and click **OK.**

    d. In the **PDF Optimizer** dialog box, in the left pane, verify that the **Images** check box is checked.

    e. In the **Color Images** section, in the **Downsample** text box next to the drop-down list, triple-click and type *100*

    f. In the **Grayscale Images** section, in the **Downsample** text box next to the drop-down list, triple-click and type *100*

---

2. Optimize the Discard Objects settings in the **PDF Optimizer** dialog box.

    a. In the left pane, select **Discard Objects** to display the discard objects settings.

    b. In the right pane, verify that the **Discard all alternate images** check box is checked.

    c. Check the **Discard embedded print settings** check box.

    d. Check the **Discard bookmarks** check box.

---

3. Optimize the Discard User Data settings.

    a. In the left pane, select **Discard User Data** to display the discard user related information settings.

    b. In the right pane, check the **Discard document information and metadata** check box.

    c. Check the **Discard file attachments** check box and click **OK.**

    d. In the **Save Optimized As** dialog box, in the **File name** text box, type *Employee Benefits_optimized*

---

e.   Click **Save** to save the optimized document.

f.   In the **Conversion Warnings** message box, click **OK.**

g.   In Windows Explorer, navigate to the C:\084548Data\Converting PDF Files folder.

h.   In the **Open** dialog box, from the **Views** drop-down menu, choose **Details.**

i.   Observe that the size of the optimized file is much smaller than that of the original.

j.   From the **Views** drop-down menu, choose **List.**

k.   Close the **Open** dialog box.

l.   Close the Employee Benefits_optimized.pdf file.

TOPIC B
Convert PDF Files to Other Formats

You optimized PDF documents to reduce their size for quick sharing and use across applications. You may also need to convert PDF documents to other file formats facilitating sharing of information across multiple applications. In this topic, you will convert a PDF document to other file formats.

Many options in Acrobat allow you to share information across formats and applications. By converting PDF files to other formats, you can enable users who do not have access to Acrobat® X Pro or Reader to obtain information that may be useful to them from other applications.

Export File Formats

You can export or convert PDF documents to multiple formats, and then open and use those files in other applications. The available formats include both text and image formats. You can export a PDF document to formats such as plain text, RTF, Microsoft Word, Excel, or accessible text, while retaining the layouts, fonts, tables, and formatting to facilitate better use of information. Accessible text follows the reading order preferences defined in the **Preferences** dialog box that control how PDF documents appear on screen and how they are viewed by on-screen readers or users who have visual disabilities. However, the converted file may not be similar to the source file and some coding information may be lost during the conversion process.

You can also convert a PDF document to image formats such as JPEG, TIFF, and PNG.

File Format	Description
JPEG	(Joint Photographic Experts Group) Compresses images maintaining acceptable levels of quality and file size.
JPEG 2000	Compresses images at a lower resolution compared to JPEG.
TIFF	(Tagged Image File Format) Stores images and is used by image-manipulating applications, publishing software, scanning, faxing, word processing, and optical character recognition software applications.
PNG	(Portable Network Graphics) Transfers images over the Internet. It also allows you to reconstruct exact data from the compressed data. It was developed to replace the GIF format.
Word Document	Saves the PDF in the DOCX format as a Word document.
Word 97-2003 Document	Saves the PDF in the DOC format as a Word document.
Microsoft Excel Workbook	Saves the PDF in the XLSX format as an Excel sheet.
XML Spreadsheet 2003	Saves the PDF in the XML format as an XML document.
PDF/A	Applies PDF/A, an ISO conversion standard, for long-term archiving of PDF documents. During PDF conversion, the file that is being processed is checked against the specified ISO standard. If it does not meet the standard, you are prompted to either cancel the conversion or create a noncompliant file.

File Format	Description
PDF/X	Applies PDF/X, an ISO standard, to graphic content exchange. During PDF conversion, the file being processed is checked against the specified ISO standard. If it does not meet the standard, you are prompted to either cancel the conversion or create a noncompliant file.
PDF/E	Applies PDF/E, an ISO standard, for the interactive exchange of engineering documents. During PDF conversion, the file being processed is checked against the specified ISO standard. If it does not meet the standard, you are prompted to either cancel the conversion or create a noncompliant file.
Rich Text Format	Converts a PDF document to the RTF format, a standard format for exchanging content between text-editing applications.
Encapsulated PostScript	Renders an image or drawing in a graphics file format. It also creates files with the EPS extension.
PostScript	Describe pages in the electronic and desktop publishing sectors. It also creates files with the .ps extension. It is chiefly used in printing.
HTML Web Page	Converts a PDF document to a web page. The HTML file and all associated files such as JPEG images, FLA files, cascading style sheets, text files, image maps, and forms are included in the conversion process. The resulting PDF behaves much like the original web page.
XML 1.0	Converts PDF documents to XML documents allowing simplicity and usability over the Internet.
Text (Accessible)	Converts PDF documents to text documents that contain no images or multimedia objects, though the text version has alternate descriptions for such objects.
Text (Plain)	Converts PDF documents to text documents.

How to Convert PDF Files to Other Formats

Procedure Reference: Convert a PDF Document to a Different File Format

To convert a PDF document to a different file format:

1. Open the PDF document.
2. Save the document as a Word document or JPEG file.
   - Choose **File→Save As→Microsoft Word→Microsoft Document** or;
   - Choose **File→Save As→Image→JPEG.**
3. In the **Save As** dialog box, navigate to the desired location.
4. If necessary, in the **File name** text box, specify a file name.
5. Click **Save** to save the document as a Word document or JPEG file.

ACTIVITY 8-2
Converting PDF Documents to Other Formats

Data Files:

C:\084548Data\Converting PDF Files\Employee Benefits.pdf

Before You Begin:

The Employee Benefits.pdf is open.

Scenario:

You want to convert the Employee Benefits.pdf file to the Microsoft Word format that you can share it with other staff members in your organization. You want it as an Microsoft Word file in order to allow your employees to suggest any required changes.

1. Save the file as a Word document and view it.

   a. Choose **File→Save As→Microsoft Word→Word Document.**

   b. In the **Save As** dialog box, in the **Save as type** drop-down list, verify that **Word Document (*.docx)** is selected.

   c. Click **Save** to save it as a Word document.

   d. In Windows Explorer, navigate to the C:\084548Data\Converting PDF Files folder.

   e. Double-click the **Employee Benefits.docx** file to open it in the Microsoft Word 2010 application.

   f. View the contents of the file.

2. Close the files and applications.

   a. Close the Microsoft Word application.

   b. Close Windows Explorer.

   c. Close the Employee Benefits.pdf file.

   d. Choose **File→Exit** to close the Acrobat X Pro application.

Lesson 8 Follow-up

In this lesson, you optimized and converted a PDF file to other formats. Optimization helps reduce the size of PDF documents, and converting or exporting PDF documents helps in sharing information.

1. **Do you think optimization will be useful for you? Why?**

2. **Why do you need to convert a PDF document to other file formats?**

Follow-up

In this course, you used Acrobat X Pro to create, access, modify, and secure PDF documents. You also worked with multiple documents, initiated a review process, and participated in PDF reviews. These skills will enable you to share information in a portable format while ensuring that your audience use the information as intended.

1. **What do you think is the best way for creating PDF documents?**

2. **What kind of modifications would you like to make in your PDF documents?**

3. **What according to you are the benefits of using PDF documents?**

What's Next?

Adobe® Acrobat® X Pro: Level 2 is the next course in this series. In this course, you will use Acrobat® X Pro to convert technical documents to PDF files, enhance and control PDF content accessibility, customize PDF documents for interactive use online, and prepare PDFs for commercial printing.

A | Setting Scanner Preferences

Lesson Time: 15 minutes

Objectives:

In this lesson, you will set the scanner preferences and scan a document.

You will:

● Scan a paper document and convert it to PDF.

Introduction

Sometimes you may have to scan a document to use it on your system. In this lesson, you will scan a document and convert it to a PDF.

Often, information is available in the paper format only. You may not be in a position to share document information with others because of cost factors. In such cases, scanning the document and converting it to a PDF will help you to share it electronically.

TOPIC A
Scan a Document

You have to send a paper document in the electronic format. In this topic, you will scan a document.

By scanning paper documents, you can share contents electronically. This helps you to make your information reach a wider audience quickly.

Scanning Options

You can create an Adobe PDF file from a paper document using a scanner. Before scanning the document, you need to specify the scanner settings appropriate for the kind of document to be scanned. You can run the Optical Character Recognition (OCR) software on the document so that the PDF generated is searchable and editable. You can also scan color and monochrome documents simultaneously with automatic color identification. In addition, using the scanning options, you can cut file size by nearly 50%, while improving the rendering of images. You can also select a basic color mode and specify the settings for scanning a paper document.

The OCR Software

The OCR software examines sequences of characters instead of words or phrases while scanning a document. When you run OCR on a scanned output, Acrobat examines bitmaps of text and substitutes words and characters for the bitmap areas. You can use Acrobat to identify text with better OCR technology in scanned documents that have already been converted to PDF. The OCR software enables you to search, correct, and copy text for reuse in other authoring applications from a scanned PDF. The text can also be exported into Microsoft Word and Excel. The **Adobe ClearScan** option can be used to create fonts to replicate the visual appearance of a scanned document after OCR.

The Custom Scan Dialog Box

The **Custom Scan** dialog box has three sections containing options for defining the scan settings.

Section	Allows You To
Input	Specify options such as the scanner to be used, the sides to be scanned, color mode, resolution, paper size, width, and height. Set a prompt for scanning more pages during the scanning process.
Output	Specify options to create a PDF document or append the scanned paper document to an existing PDF document or portfolio.
Document Settings	Optimize the scanned PDF for smaller file size or high quality. You can also specify the settings for making the PDF file searchable, PDF/A-1b compliant, and also add metadata.

How to Scan a Document

Procedure Reference: Create a PDF Document from Scanned Pages

To scan a paper document and convert it to a PDF file:

 You need to connect a scanner to your computer after inserting the paper document to be scanned.

1. Open Adobe Acrobat X Pro application.
2. Choose **File→Create→PDF from Scanner→Black & White Document.**

 Acrobat will scan the document and display it with the default name **Untitled.pdf.**

3. In the **Acrobat Scan** message box, perform the desired action.
    *   Select the **Scan is Complete** option to complete the scan process.
    *   Select the **Scan more pages (sheet 2)** option to scan additional pages.
    *   Select the **Scan reverse sides (of sheet 1)** option to scan the reverse side of a document.
4. Click OK to close the **Acrobat Scan** message box.
5. Choose **File→Save As→PDF** to save the document.
6. In the **Save As** dialog box, in the File name text box, specify the file name.
7. Click **Save.**

Specify Scanner Settings

Before creating a PDF from scanned pages, you can specify the scanner settings to provide the desired look and feel for your document. These settings are available in the **Custom Scan** dialog box.

Section/Option	Allows You To
Scanner	Select the scanning device.
Sides	Specify the side of the document to be scanned.
Color Mode	Select the desired color mode.
Resolution	Select a resolution supported by the scanner.
Paper Size	Select the desired paper size or specify the custom paper size in the **Width** and **Height** text boxes.
Output	Specify whether to create a PDF document or append the scanned paper document to an existing PDF document or portfolio.
Multiple files	Create multiple PDF copies from a single set of papers.

Section/Option	Allows You To
More Options	Specify the desired additional settings.
Make Searchable (Run OCR)	Make text and images in the PDF searchable and selectable, and also convert text images to normal text.
Add Metadata	Include information about the scanned document to the PDF file.

The ClearScan Option for Accurate OCR

The **ClearScan** option is available in the **Recognize Text-Settings** dialog box. Selecting this option ensures that the PDF document that you generate displays the text and images in a format that resembles the original text and graphics. It also preserves the page background by using a low resolution.

Procedure Reference: Define Preferences for a Scanned Document

To define preferences for a scanned document:

1. Choose **File→Create→PDF from Scanner→Custom Scan** to display the **Custom Scan** dialog box.

2. In the **Custom Scan** dialog box, specify the desired settings.

   - In the **Input** section, perform the desired action.

     ■ From the **Scanner** drop-down list, select the scanner device connected to the computer.

      You can click **Options** to specify the desired mode of data transfer, specify a user interface, and if necessary, select the option to create positive images from the paper document.

     ■ From the **Sides** drop-down list, select the desired option to specify whether you want a single side or double side to be scanned.

     ■ From the **Color Mode** drop-down list, select a basic color mode.

     ■ From the **Resolution** drop-down list, select the desired resolution.

     ■ From the **Paper Size** drop-down list, select a paper size and in the **Width** and **Height** text boxes, specify the desired custom width and height.

     ■ Check the **Prompt for scanning more pages** check box to scan additional pages at the time of scanning.

   - In the **Output** section, perform the desired action.

     ■ Select the **New PDF Document** option to create a PDF document.

      You can check the **Multiple files** check box to create multiple files from multiple paper documents. You can click **More Options** and specify various options to create a PDF portfolio of the files, the number of pages for each file, and a filename prefix for the files.

- ■ Select the **Append to existing file or portfolio** option to append the scanned document to a new PDF or portfolio.
- ● In the **Document Settings** section, perform the desired action.
  - ■ Check the **Optimize Scanned PDF** check box to compress and filter the images in the scanned PDF.

 You can click **Options** and customize the settings for higher quality images, smaller file sizes, or scanning preferences.

  - ■ Adjust the slider to set the balance point between file size and quality.
  - ■ Check the **Make Searchable (Run OCR)** check box to convert images in the PDF to searchable and selectable text.

 You can click **Options** to specify the language for the OCR engine to identify characters or select **PDF Output Style** option to determine the type of PDF document to produce.

  - ■ Check the **Make PDF/A-1b compliant** check box to make the PDF conform to the ISO standards for PDF/A-1b.
  - ■ Check the **Add Metadata** check box to add metadata to the PDF document.
3. If necessary, click **Defaults** to set the default settings.
4. Click **Scan** to scan the document.

ACTIVITY A-1
Scan a Document

Before You Begin:

1. Ensure that a scanner is connected to your computer.

2. Ensure you have a hard copy of a document containing at least one page.

Scenario:

You have a hard copy of a document and would like to send it to your colleague. You decide to scan and convert the scanned file to a PDF document. After having converted it to a PDF document, you want to save the scanned document.

---

1. Scan the document.

    a. Open the Adobe Acrobat X Pro application

    b. Insert the document page in the scanner.

    c. Choose **File→Create→PDF from Scanner→Black & White Document.**

    d. Observe that a message box displays that scanning is in progress.

    e. In the **Acrobat Scan** message box, select the **Scan is Complete** option and click **OK.**

---

2. Save the scanned document.

    a. Choose **File→Save As→PDF** to save it as a PDF document.

    b. In the **File name** text box, type a file name for the PDF document.

    c. Click **Save.**

Lesson Labs

Lesson labs are provided as an additional learning resource for this course. The labs may or may not be performed as part of the classroom activities. Your instructor will consider setup issues, classroom timing issues, and instructional needs to determine which labs are appropriate for you to perform, and at what point during the class. If you do not perform the labs in class, your instructor can tell you if you can perform them independently as self-study, and if there are any special setup requirements.

Lesson 1 Lab 1

Accessing Information in a PDF Document

Data Files:

C:\084548Data\Accessing PDF Documents\Celebrations.pdf

Scenario:

Your manager gave you the Celebrations.pdf file and asked you to provide feedback about the file and make necessary changes to it. You are provided with a system which has the Acrobat X Pro application installed. Before actually starting off with the review, you want to familiarize yourself with the Acrobat X Pro interface because you have no prior experience working with that application.

---

1.   Open the Celebrations.pdf file from the C:\084548Data\Accessing PDF Documents folder and display each set of pages as a spread so that you can view the entire spread within the document window.

---

2.   View all the page spreads and browse through the document.

---

3.   Explore the options in the **Navigation Pane.**

---

4.   Explore the toolbar options.

---

5.   Close the Celebrations.pdf file.

Lesson 2 Lab 1

Combining Files to Create a PDF Portfolio

Data Files:

C:\084548Data\Creating PDF Documents\Christmas.docx, C:\084548Data\Creating PDF Documents\Thanksgiving.docx, C:\084548Data\Creating PDF Documents\Independence Day.pdf

Scenario:

You are given the responsibility of creating a marketing brochure for your organization describing the various festival holidays. Your colleague has already developed the content using the Microsoft Word application. You need to create a single file with all the information about the festivals so that it can be sent to the clients as a complete document. You also need to generate a PDF document of your company's website.

1. Open the Christmas.docx and Thanksgiving.docx files from the C:\084548Data\Creating PDF Documents folder.

2. Generate a PDF of the Christmas.docx and Thanksgiving.docx files using the Standard conversion setting and save them as ***Christmas.pdf*** and ***Thanksgiving.pdf*** respectively.

3. Combine the Christmas.docx, Independence Day.pdf, and Thanksgiving.docx files from the C:\084548Data\Creating PDF Documents folder to create a single PDF portfolio.

4. Save the PDF portfolio as ***Celebrations.pdf*** and close it.

5. Convert all pages on the Our Global Company website to a single PDF document.

6. View the generated PDF and close it.

Lesson 3 Lab 1

Adding PDF Navigation Aids

Data Files:

C:\084548Data\Navigating to Specific Content\Celebrations.pdf

Scenario:

You are working on the Celebrations document, and you want to include bookmarks for each subheading so that it will be easy to navigate to a specific topic of interest. You want to add links that will allow others to easily navigate through the file.

---

1. Open the Celebrations.pdf file from the C:\084548Data\Navigating to Specific Content in a PDF Document folder.

---

2. Create bookmarks that navigate to each heading in the document.

---

3. Display the contents in the Actual Size view.

---

4. Use the **Bookmarks** panel and nest the subheading bookmarks below the "Holidays" main heading. Apply bold formatting to the main heading bookmark.

---

5. Create a destination that displays page IV in the Fit Width view, with the "Thanksgiving" heading at the top of the window. Name the destination as ***Thanksgiving.***

---

6. On page 1, at the bottom of the page, for the text "THE MOST CELEBRATED DAYS IN AMERICA," create a link which navigates to the "Thanksgiving" destination. Format the link to display a medium-thick line, with a blue underline.

---

7. On page 2, create links for each heading.

---

8. Test the new navigation features you have added.

---

9. Save the file as ***My Celebrations.pdf*** and close the file.

Lesson 4 Lab 1

Modifying the Celebrations Document

Data Files:

C:\084548Data\Updating PDF Documents\Celebrations.pdf, C:\084548Data\Updating PDF Documents\Independence Day.pdf

Scenario:

You need to include information about the American Independence day in the Celebrations.pdf file. The information is available to you as a separate PDF file. You want to include it at the end of the Celebrations document. You also want to insert appropriate header and footer information, and include a watermark and a background to the document.

1. Open the Celebrations.pdf file from the C:\084548Data\Updating PDF Documents folder.

2. Include the content in the Independence Day.pdf file as the last page in the Celebrations.pdf file.

3. In the Celebrations.pdf file, include the text *"American Celebrations"* as the right header information. Add the page number and the text *"Compiled by D Catherine"* as the left and right footer information.

4. Add a watermark to all document pages with the text *"Festive Season."* Set the text to display at a 45 degree angle and adjust its opacity so that the text behind the watermark is visible.

5. In the **Page Thumbnails** panel, change the page numbering of the Celebrations.pdf file such that pages I–IV begin with a new section starting from 1 to 5.

6. Save the file as *My Celebrations.pdf.*

Lesson 5 Lab 1

Managing Multiple PDF Documents

Data Files:

C:\084548Data\Working with Multiple PDF Documents\Celebrations.pdf

Scenario:

You have the Celebrations.pdf file and want to plan for your vacation. You want to collect information about the details included in the document. You want to distribute it among your friends and to ensure that they do not tamper with the original document. You want to hide some information from the document that others cannot view them and add Bates numbering to the documents.

---

1. Open the Celebrations.pdf file from the C:\084548Data\Working with Multiple PDF Documents folder.

---

2. Search for the word "orange" in the Celebrations.pdf file.

---

3. On page 3, redact the second line in the second paragraph.

---

4. Set security preferences to the Celebrations.pdf file by specifying the password as *password1234.*

---

5. Save the file as *My Celebrations_Redacted.pdf.*

---

6. Add Bates numbering with a prefix *LEV* to the Celebrations.pdf file.

---

7. Save the file as *Celebrations_Bates.pdf.*

---

8. Close all the files.

Lesson 6 Lab 1

Reviewing and Comparing the Celebrations Document

Data Files:

C:\084548Data\Reviewing PDF Documents\Celebrations.pdf

Scenario:

You created a brochure about the festival holidays celebrated in the US. Before sending it out to your colleagues in your organization, you want to send it for a review.

---

1. Open the Celebrations.pdf file from the C:\084548Data\Reviewing PDF Documents folder.

---

2. Save a copy of the Celebrations.pdf file as **Celebrations Review.pdf** file.

---

3. In the **Identity** category of the **Preferences** dialog box, specify your name and email details.

---

4. Make changes to the Celebrations Review.pdf file using the tools in the **Comment** panel.

---

5. Compare the Celebrations.pdf and the Celebrations Review.pdf files.

---

6. Save and close all the files.

Lesson 7 Lab 1

Signing the Celebrations Brochure Digitally

Data Files:

C:\084548Data\Validating PDF Documents\Celebrations.pdf

Scenario:

The Celebrations.pdf file is ready for distribution to your clients. Given the exclusive nature of the information that is present, you need to validate it for authenticity.

1. Open the Celebrations.pdf file from the C:\084548Data\Validating PDF Documents folder.

2. Digitally sign the document as **Cathy** of Rudison Technologies at the footer section of page i.

3. Set the password for the document as **password.**

4. Validate the digital ID.

5. Save the file as **My Celebrations.pdf.**

Lesson 8 Lab 1

Optimizing and Converting a PDF File

Data Files:

C:\084548Data\Converting PDF Files\Celebrations.pdf

Scenario:

You have got a copy of the Celebrations document for distributing to the employees in your organization. You want to compress the file size and then send the file in the Microsoft Word format to all the employees.

1. Open the Celebrations.pdf file from the C:\084548Data\Converting PDF Files folder.

2. Set the optimization settings for the Celebrations.pdf file using the **PDF Optimizer** dialog box.

3. Save the document as ***Celebrations_Optimized.pdf.***

4. Convert the file to a Microsoft Word document.

5. Save the Microsoft Word document as ***Celebrations_Optimized.docx.***

Solutions

Lesson 1

Activity 1-1

2. **Which command would you use to convert a document from any application to a PDF document?**

    a) The Save As command

    ✓ b) The Print command

    c) The Page Setup command

    d) The Print Preview command

Activity 1-3

4. **Which toolbar contains the tools to browse through a PDF document?**

    a) The Tasks toolbar

    b) The Select & Zoom toolbar

    ✓ c) The Page Navigation toolbar

    d) The Page Display toolbar

Lesson 2

Activity 2-4

2. **Which option helps you to create a PDF of a Microsoft Outlook email message?**

    ✓ a) Create New PDF

    b) Change Conversion Settings

    c) Setup Automatic Archival

    d) Selected Messages

Glossary

Acrobat PDFMaker conversion settings
Collections of settings that determine the characteristics of the PDF files you generate.

Adobe Acrobat X Pro window
A window that consists of interface elements that help you create PDF documents.

authoring application
An application in which the content is authored.

bookmark
A text entry link that you can click to navigate to a location in a PDF document.

comments
Tools used by a reviewer to state an opinion or give a suggestion about content in a document.

destination
The end point of a link which enables navigation paths to be set across a collection of PDF documents.

digital ID
An identification that allows you to create a digital signature containing a name, an email address, a serial number, and an expiration date.

digital signature
Information that is used to uniquely identify an individual.

link
An item which helps in navigating to a different location within the PDF document.

metadata
Data which provides additional information about specific text information in the document.

optimization
A process of reducing the size of a PDF document by removing embedded fonts, compressing images, and discarding unwanted objects and data.

PDF
(Portable Document Format) A file format created by Adobe Acrobat which is primarily used to document any information that retains the original layout of the document.

Read mode
A mode which displays maximum view of the screen by hiding the toolbars and Task pane.

security envelope
An encryption method that allows to encrypt documents as file attachments which can be sent via email.

security policy
A set of security settings that are created to protect and authenticate a document.

stamps

Tools that inform users about the status of a
PDF document.

Index

A

Acrobat
  collaboration workflows, 122
Acrobat PDFMaker conversion settings, 24
Adobe Acrobat X Pro window, 6
Adobe LiveCycle Rights Management server, 145
Adobe PDF compatibility settings, 25
Adobe PDF printer, 29
Adobe PDF printing preferences, 30
advanced search options, 113
annotations, 131
authoring application, 2

B

backgrounds, 89
bates numbering, 114
bookmarks, 57
Bookmarks
  adding actions, 60
  changing destination, 60
  changing the formatting, 60
  creating, 59
Bookmarks panel, 58

C

Combine Files dialog box, 41
comments, 130
Compare Documents feature, 138
compatibility options, 109
Content panel, 83
converting a mail folder to PDF, 37
converting Lotus Notes messages to PDF, 36
converting web page selections to PDF, 34

converting web pages to PDF, 33
Create PDF Portfolio dialog box, 43

D

destinations, 65
digital IDs, 144, 155
  creating, 149
  exporting, 150
digital signatures, 144
  verifying, 156
document security options, 104
drawing markups, 132

E

Edit Document Text tool, 84
email-based reviews, 124
export file formats, 166

F

Find toolbar, 53
font embedding and substitution, 25
footers, 89
Full Screen mode, 15

G

grabber bar, 8

H

headers, 89

I

image formats, 95

L

links, 65

live collaboration, 124

M

metadata, 112

O

optimization, 160

P

page numbering, 75
Page Thumbnails panel, 75
Pages section, 74
PDF, 2
  adding review comments, 135
  adding stamps, 134
  archiving, 139
  converting to other file formats, 97
  cropping the pages., 79
  deleting pages, 77
  digitally signing, 150
  exporting images, 98
  extracting pages, 96
  inserting pages, 77
  rearranging pages, 78
  removing security settings, 109
  restricting access, 107
  splitting into multiple files, 78
PDF Optimizer dialog box, 160
PDF Portfolio, 22

R

Read mode, 15

redaction, 105
  applying to sensitive content, 106
  options, 106
resizing, 14
review tracker, 123

S

Search window, 52, 53
security envelopes, 145
security methods, 148
security policies, 148
shared reviews, 123
Sign & Certify section, 146
Signatures panel, 146
stamps, 129

T

toolbars
  customizing, 9
Typewriter toolbar, 84

U

using content in other applications, 96

W

watermarks, 89

Z

zooming, 13